Journal of PRAYER

An Anthology

Compiled by Richard A. Hasler

Judson Press ® Valley Forge

*To my parents, Charles and Grace Hasler; my wife's
parents, Ellsworth and Katie Sandherr; my
daughter, Karen, and her husband, Mike Kelly; my son,
Rick, and his wife, Cindy; and above all to my wife, Arlene,
without whose inspiration and encouragement this book
would not have been completed.*

JOURNAL OF PRAYER

Copyright © 1982
Judson Press, Valley Forge, PA 19481

Library of Congress Cataloging—in Publication Data
Main entry under title:

Journal of prayer.

Includes bibliographical references and index.
1. Prayer—Quotations, maxims, etc.   I. Hasler,
Richard A.
BV205.J68   248.3'2   82-235
ISBN 0-8170-0965-5   AACR2

The name JUDSON PRESS is registered as a trademark in the U.S. Patent
Office. Printed in the U.S.A. ⊕

Contents

Introduction

"Nothing costs so much as free grace" wrote P. T. Forsyth in his discussion of prayer.[1] I know what he means. The practice of prayer has not been easy for me. Prayer involves discipline, struggle, and sacrifice. I cannot simply pray by myself. I need help, especially in my low moments when prayer seems next to impossible.

At such times I have turned to the writings of men and women who have excelled in articulating their own encounters with God in prayer. To be sure, I have consulted the devotional classics written by Augustine, Teresa of Avila, Martin Luther, John Bunyan, David Brainerd, John Woolman, and other spiritual guides. In more recent years, however, I have concentrated upon twentieth-century interpreters of prayer, such as P.T. Forsyth, quoted at the outset. I picked up his little book, *The Soul of Prayer,* for seventy-five cents at a used-book store more than twenty years ago. To this day I continue to copy quotations from the book and insert them in my own journal. The habit begun with the reading of Forsyth's book has extended to numerous other writers who have given me fresh stimulus and direction.

The treasury of prayer that follows includes selections from a wide variety of twentieth-century authors—Protestant, Roman Catholic, Eastern Orthodox, and Jewish. The quotations are grounded in the realism of the biblical understanding of prayer, in contrast to much of the "pop" literature on prayer today that is simplistic, sentimental, and self-centered. Although a rich diversity of expression will be noted in the collection, all writers testify to the same reality of having been grasped by the grace of God in prayer.

Reading the book may be approached from two angles. Pastors, educators, and other religious leaders may wish to use the material as a topical reference book to assist them in their important responsibilities related to worship and classroom teaching. Twelve major facets of prayer are covered: preparation, adoration, confession, thanksgiving, petition, intercession, silence, persistence, communion, surrender, recollection, and action.

Or the book may be used as a journal of prayer and read daily throughout the course of the year. Each of the quotations contains an incisive thought to set the tone for the day. I recommend that you read every selection slowly, deliberately, prayerfully, and assimilate the meaning into your own life.

You are invited to begin your own exploration and to anticipate that in this costly labor of prayer you too will know the exhilarating experience of being "found by God."

1

Preparation

Found by God

"We move into the deepest kind of interior prayer in order that we may be found by God, recognized by the Lord of our lives, and loved into being."[1]

—Madeleine L'Engle, *"The Gift of Prayer"*

Prayer Is Grace

"Prayer is a grace, an offer of God."[2]

—Karl Barth, *Prayer According to the Catechisms of the Reformation*

We Do Not Generate Grace

"We do not project or generate grace. Nor do we initiate the redemptive order—process—which, when we let it, sweeps

7

into its course our scarred lives, our prayers, and our concerns for others."[3]

—Douglas Steere, *Dimensions of Prayer*

Long Before We Came to Him

"It matters little what form of prayer we adopt or how many words we use, what matters is the faith which lays hold on God and touches the heart of the Father who knew us long before we came to him."[4]

—Dietrich Bonhoeffer, *The Cost of Discipleship*

The Reality That Governs Our Destiny

"The central Jewish prayer is not really a prayer at all, in the conventional sense. . . . It is called the 'Shema' because it opens 'Listen!' or 'Hear!'. This is not said quietly, but loudly. God does not have to be told that he is One—presumably He knows it—but our fellow Jews do. We remind our relatives, the family of Israel, of the reality which governs our destiny. The key Jewish prayer is therefore really not said to God at all, it is said to ourselves, and above all, we say it at each other. We have publicly stated the truth, and fulfilled our duty. We have put the reality of God's Kingdom above all its competitors. This is prayer!"[5]

—Lionel Blue, *To Heaven with Scribes and Pharisees: The Jewish Path to God*

To Be Met by Another

"In so many tentative and halting ways, we learn through the life of prayer what it is to be met by Another, and to trust that Other by whom we are met."[6]

—James E. Griffiss, *A Silent Path to God*

What Is Best in Our Lives

"However hard our work, we recognize, when we are honest, that we are not self-made creatures, and that what is best in our lives comes by grace rather than by our own deserts."[7]

—Elton Trueblood, *The Lord's Prayers*

God Is Ever Seeking

"The great thing to remember is that God, being Who He is, is more ready to hear than we to pray, more eager to give than we to receive, more active to find us than we to find Him. God is ever seeking man: His ear is more sensitive to the words, His heart to the desires, of men than the aspen leaf to the summer breeze, than the compass needle to the call of the poles."[8]

—Charles Henry Brent, *Things That Matter*

The Anti-Consumer Prayer

"We can say that the model furnished by Jesus is the anti-consumer prayer par excellence. It is centered on God's needs, not ours."[9]

—Jacques Ellul, *Prayer and Modern Man*

The Eternal Song of the Other

"The song *is put into* our mouths, for the Singer of all songs is singing with us. It is not we that sing; it is the Eternal Song of the Other, who sings in us, who sings unto us, and through us into the world."[10]

—Thomas R. Kelly, *A Testament of Devotion*

The First Condition
"The first condition for prayer is the recognition of a *need* that cannot be solved by oneself."[11]

> —Michael H. Crosby, *Thy Will Be Done: Praying the Our Father as Subversive Activity*

Prayer Is . . . Original Research
"Prayer is for the religious life what original research is for science—by it we get direct contact with reality."[12]

> —P. T. Forsyth, *The Soul of Prayer*

Our Job . . . God's Business
"Our job is to put ourselves at God's disposal by the discipline of regularity, by faithfulness to our rule, and by the use of that common sense without which we can't do anything. But there our job ends. What happens when we pray is God's business, not ours. God will give us what he knows is best. And what is best we can see in the life of Jesus, in His joy and peace and stillness and confidence and trust. And also in His passion, His bloody sweat, His death and resurrection."[13]

> —H. A. Williams, *The Simplicity of Prayer*

Not a Landlord-Tenant Arrangement
"To the pagans, God was a celestial landlord who had to be worried into fixing things up for them. They made sure that God was informed (in high-sounding dignified language, of course) of the terrible mess that his earthly estate was in and how badly that part of it in which they lived needed patching up. . . . On the other hand, the kingdom citizen was not on a landlord-tenant arrangement; it was a Father-son relationship. He quietly trusted the Father to anticipate and supply

all his physical needs while he devoted himself completely to the accomplishing of the Father's work on earth. . . . His desire was not to use God but to be used by him." [14]

> —Clarence Jordan, *Sermon on the Mount*

Spiritual Exercises

"We need spiritual exercises if we are going to deepen our knowledge of God, but they must be our own exercises. . . . At least once a year we need to take time to reflect on where we are and what our goals are, and then decide on the disciplines that will help us reach them." [15]

> —Elizabeth O'Connor, *Journey Inward, Journey Outward*

No Settled Rule

"There is no settled rule. Everyone must find for himself the way that leads him deepest into the Presence." [16]

> —Arthur Gossip, *In the Secret Place of the Most High*

Your Method

"Any method, absolutely any method is *your* method, if you find it opens the doors toward heaven and helps you gain contact with God. And it is not your method, no matter who does it, if it does not succeed in doing that." [17]

> —Frank Laubach, *Channels of Spiritual Power*

The Sense of Time

"We can pray to God only if we are established in a state

of stability and inner peace face to face with God, and these things release us from the sense of time—not objective time, the kind we watch—but the subjective sense that time is running fast and that we have no time left."[18]

—Anthony Bloom, *Beginning
to Pray*

Common and Private Prayer
"Common prayer does not dispense us from private prayer. The one sustains the other. Let us each day take time to renew our personal intimacy with Jesus Christ."[19]

—Roger Schutz, *The Rule of
Taizé*

Take Trouble to Pray
"Love to pray—feel often during the day the need for prayer, and take trouble to pray. Prayer enlarges the heart until it is capable of containing God's gift of himself."[20]

—Mother Teresa, *A Gift for God*

Take the Time Alone
"Someone has said that the lives of most persons are like jewelry stores where some trickster has mixed up the price tags. The diamonds are priced at next to nothing and some worthless baubles at thousands of dollars. Unless we stop business as usual and take stock, we are likely to end up in bankruptcy. So long as the store is crowded with people, there is no chance of taking inventory and putting things to rights. We must close the doors and take the time alone."[21]

—Morton T. Kelsey, *The Other
Side of Silence*

A Time When We Get Still

"Our discipline of prayer is a channel by which we receive the gift of God's very being. This is not merely a rule that we keep—it is a time when we get still. It is a time when we let God address us, command us, penetrate us, exercise his sovereign will over us."[22]

—Gordon Cosby, *Handbook for Mission Groups*

Prayer Takes Time Seriously

"Christians think that time is part of the goodness of creation, but it has been given a special holiness by the coming of Jesus as a child of time. They believe that the way of life he commended is a way of personally experiencing the sanctification of time. Prayer, being exercise towards this experience, takes time seriously, indeed keeps it in the mind almost continually but bathed in a certain sanctifying light. Morning and evening, the week, the months and the year all influence the content and movement of Christian prayer and so doing make themselves felt more, not less, as part of the presence of time."[23]

—J. Neville Ward, *The Use of Praying*

Do We Really Want the Quiet Time?

"Sometimes these moments open up most naturally in the evening. For some, they seem more fruitful in the early hours before other lives make traffic in the mind. They may come at unexpected places in the day's activity. But the important thing is to want them—to want them regularly—and to let God know that we will be ready whenever he brings us to these havens of quiet along the routes of our daily lives. The vital question is not, 'What will we do in the quiet time?' It isn't 'When will we keep the quiet time?' What matters most is, 'Do we really want the quiet time?'"[24]

—Charlie Shedd, *Time for All Things*

The Early Dawn
    "Forever let me be a child of the early dawn."[25]

                            —Kagawa, *Kagawa*

Not the Words but the Attitude
    "The formal manner of addressing God in King James'–style English is no more sacred than current expressions we use in today's English. It is not the words we use, but the attitude we bring to prayer that matters."[26]

                            —Orien Johnson, *Becoming
                            Transformed*

To Affirm Life
    "To pray is to affirm life. It is to stay bound up with God's life regardless of how many questions lie upon the ground unanswered."[27]

                            —James Angell, *When God
                            Made You, He Knew What He
                            Was Doing*

Meaning and Living
    "We cannot fall on our knees and cry with any meaning: 'O, God, O Father, O Judge, O Savior,' if our whole lives are not lived in the context of the meaning of these exclamations."[28]

                            —Reuel Howe, *Herein Is Love*

A Wonderful Reduction of Eternity
    "Prayer is always a wonderful reduction of eternity to the dimension of a moment in time, a reduction of the eternal

wisdom to the dimension of human knowledge, feeling and understanding, a reduction of eternal Love to the dimension of the human heart, which at times is incapable of absorbing its riches and seems to break."[29]

—Karol Wojtyla (Pope John Paul
II), *Sign of Contradiction*

Unlimited Possibilties

"Deep in every one of us lies the tendency to pray. If we allow it to remain merely a tendency, it becomes nothing but a selfish, unintelligent, occasional cry of need. But understood and disciplined, it reveals possibilities whose limits never have been found."[30]

—Harry Emerson Fosdick, *The
Meaning of Prayer*

Three Kinds of Prayer

"There are three kinds of souls, three kinds of prayers. One: I am a bow in your hands, Lord. Draw me lest I rot. Two: Do not overdraw me, Lord, I shall break. Three: Overdraw me, and who cares if I break!"[31]

—Nikos Kazantzakis, *Report to
Greco*

2

Adoration

The Fact of God
"The first cause of all prayer and worship . . . is the fact of God, the One Reality—half-realized by those who are 'feeling after' him, accepted with adoring delight by those who have been 'found' by him."[1]

—Olive Wyon, *Prayer*

The Only Adoration
"The only adoration which is not at the same time idolatry is adoration of God. . . . Adoration is a form of love which can safely be directed only to God. Only here may it escape the bitterness of ultimate disillusionment. Adoration may be addressed only to the 'holy'; and only God is holy."[2]

—John Yungblut, *Rediscovering Prayer*

Awful Power and Majesty of God
"If holiness and the awful power and majesty of God were present in this least auspicious of all events, this birth of a peasant's child, then there is no place or time so lowly and earthbound but that holiness can be present there too."[3]

—Frederick Buechner, *The Hungering Dark*

The Senior Partner
"God makes us covenant partners in the working out of his purposes in the world, and yet we are not equal partners. God is the senior partner and must therefore be approached in awe and reverence."[4]

—Donald G. Bloesch, *The Struggle of Prayer*

The Sense of the Ineffable
"The true source of prayer is not an emotion but an insight. It is the insight into the mystery of reality, the sense of the ineffable, that enables us to pray."[5]

—Abraham Heschel, *The Wisdom of Heschel*

One Pencil of Light
"When all your strength ought to be focused into one pencil of light pointing up through the darkness, you allow it to be dissipated in a moss fire where nothing is consumed, but *all* life is suffocated."[6]

—Dag Hammarskjöld, *Markings*

The Angelus Time
"Jean Francois Millet's famous painting, 'The Angelus,'

. . . portrays a peasant farmer and his wife pausing in their work to listen with bowed heads as the bells announcing the Angelus ring out over the fields from the church tower in the village. As they wait in silence they look to God and love him. The strain and bitterness leave their souls, and their troubles as well as their work are seen in a new light.

"We all need to have an Angelus time regularly in our lives, when through the adoration of God we can see life in a new perspective. Some period in every day when we can be still and know that he is God and love and adore him!"[7]

—Lance Webb, *The Art of Personal Prayer*

Room for Reverence

". . . when we begin to pray by saying, 'Hallowed be thy name,' we are letting the holiness, the wonder, the glory, the perfection of God himself invade our spirits and possess our minds. We are, as it were, detaching what we do from the mechanics of everyday, and creating the atmosphere of prayer. We do not then rush to our requests as though prayer was like picking up a telephone. We first realise the holy. We make room for reverence."[8]

—David Read, *Holy Common Sense*

The Sense of Awe

"The sense of awe becomes trumpet-tongued, and the sheer joy of the beauty of holiness overwhelms the mind and enlivens all the emotions with a kindling of spiritual fervor. It is at such a moment that one feels he was created to praise God and to enjoy Him forever."[9]

—Howard Thurman, *Disciplines of the Spirit*

Praising God

"Praising God is giving up idealism and becoming pragmatic. Praising God is tossing away the mumbo jumbo of technological arrogance and speaking the facts of faith. Praising God is abandoning the illusion of human control and embracing the truth of God's power."[10]

—Thomas Troeger, *Rage! Reflect. Rejoice!*

Sunny and Reverent

"One may be very solemn and very reverent. But one may also be very sunny and very reverent."[11]

—Clovis G. Chappell, *Sermons on the Lord's Prayer*

Nature's Creator

"We feel a kinship with nature and an adoration for its creator. Mountains seem to be especially significant. Grandiose and peaked, they not only point as nature's arches to the heavens, but also make us feel small in an aesthetic rather than a melancholy way. We experience our creatureliness within an awareness of the Transcendent One who transcends all limits."[12]

—William E. Hulme, *Let the Spirit In*

Why Adore God?

"To ask *why* one should adore God is like asking a lover why he adores his beloved. His only answer can be, 'Why, because she *is*.' So a man loves God, not because he has helped him or answered his prayers or forgiven him his sin, or for any gifts he has given. He loves God simply because God is God. . . . The prayer of adoration is to thank God for God!"[13]

—John B. Coburn, *Prayer and Personal Religion*

If God Really Is a Lover

"If God really is a Lover, he must delight in having those whom he loves respond to him in love and want to be with him and tell him their love."[14]

—Norman Pittenger, *Praying Today*

Cosmic Companionship

"I am convinced that the universe is under the control of a loving purpose, and that in the struggle for righteousness man has cosmic companionship. Behind the harsh appearances of the world there is a benign power."[15]

—Martin Luther King, Jr., *Strength to Love*

A Heart Wide Open

"Grant us, we pray thee, a heart wide open to all this joy and beauty, and save our souls from being so steeped in care or so darkened by passion that we pass heedless and unseeing when even the thornbush by the wayside is aflame with the glory of God."[16]

—Walter Rauschenbusch, *Prayers of the Social Awakening*

To Adore . . . Only the Echo

". . . it is so easy for us to fall in love with the gift and forget the giver. This is why there is always a danger, a subtle danger, of idolatry—to adore that which is not God, but only the echo; to fall in love with the painting and not to know the painter; to fall in love with the music and not know the heart out of which this music has come; and we, ourselves, to fall in love with our own life and yet not know from whom it has come, where it is going or how it is sustained."[17]

—Edward J. Farrell, *Prayer Is a Hunger*

We Move Away from Ourselves

"Prayer is a radical conversion of all our mental processes, because in prayer we move away from ourselves—our worries, preoccupations, and self-gratifications—and direct all that we recognize as ours to God in the simple trust that through his love all will be made new."[18]

—Henri J. Nouwen, *Clowning in Rome*

A Great Healing Process

"The man who hallows God's name, lets him be his Lord, and surrenders his life to him will be drawn quite spontaneously and before he is aware of it into a great healing process, and he becomes a new person."[19]

—Helmut Thielicke, *Our Heavenly Father: Sermons on the Lord's Prayer*

He Wanted Me

"A Christian is a tabernacle of the living God. He created me, he chose me, he came to dwell in me, because he wanted me. Now that you have known how much God is in love with you, it is natural that you spend the rest of your life radiating that love."[20]

—Mother Teresa, *A Gift for God*

The Most Selfless of All Emotions

"To worship is to quicken the conscience by the holiness of God, to feed the mind with the truth of God, to purge the imagination by the beauty of God, to open the heart to the love of God, to devote the will to the purpose of God. All this is gathered up in that emotion which most cleanses us from selfishness because it is the most selfless of all emotions—adoration."[21]

—William Temple, *Daily Readings from William Temple*

The Foregleam of Eternal Life

"To glorify God in 'wonder, love, and praise' is the fore-gleam of eternal life."[22]

—George A. Buttrick, *Prayer*

A Single Experience

"We can't—or I can't—hear the song of a bird simply as a sound. Its meaning or message ('That's a bird') comes with it inevitably—just as one can't see a familiar word in print as a merely visual pattern. The reading is as involuntary as the seeing. When the wind roars I don't just hear the roar; I 'hear the wind.' In the same way it is possible to 'read' as well as to 'have' a pleasure. Or not even 'as well as.' The distinction ought to become, and sometimes is, impossible; to receive it and to recognise its divine source are a single experience. The heavenly fruit is instantly redolent of the orchard where it grew. This sweet air whispers of the country from whence it blows. It is a message. We know we are being touched by a finger of that right hand at which there are pleasures for evermore. There need be no question of thanks or praise as a separate event, something done afterwards. To experience the tiny theophany is itself to adore."[23]

—C. S. Lewis, *Letters to Malcolm: Chiefly on Prayer*

No Dilemma

"Adoration is the unchanging heart of religion, and the only key to its mysterious truth. There is no dilemma for the adoring soul."[24]

—Evelyn Underhill, *The Evelyn Underhill Reader*

Greater than All Men's Dreams

"God will always be beyond the compass of our little,

finite minds, and He will both do and allow things that puzzle, bewilder, and affright us, but, although we don't know much *about* God, we know God in Jesus, and knowing, we can rest our minds in His infinity. . . . 'O magnify the Lord with me, and let us exalt His name together'; for He is greater than all human thought concerning Him and better than all men's dreams."[25]

> —Leslie Weatherhead, *Daily Readings from the Works of Leslie Weatherhead*

Miracles Most of Us Never See

"The world is full of miracles that most of us never see. We have not trained ourselves to look. We are like processionary caterpillars, those pathetic insects which, if led onto the lip of a fruitjar, will join ranks head-to-tail and proceed around the jar until they fall starving and exhausted to the ground. Blindly we make our way from the cradle to the grave. . . .

"It is when we see the world for what it is, a miracle in itself—a miracle filled with miracles—that prayer comes into its own."[26]

> —John Killinger, *Bread for the Wilderness, Wine for the Journey*

The Beginning and the End

"The adoration of God is the beginning and the end of all our prayer, as it is of all our life."[27]

> —John Casteel, *The Promise of Prayer*

I Look Back in Wonder

"How easy for me to live with You, O Lord! How easy for me to believe in You!

When my mind parts in bewilderment
or falters,
when the most intelligent people see no further
than this day's end
and do not know what must be done tomorrow,
You grant me the serene certitude
that You exist and that You will take care
that not all the paths of good be closed.
Atop the ridge of earthly fame,
I look back in wonder at the path
which I alone could never have found,
a wondrous path through despair to this point
from which I, too, could transmit to mankind
a reflection of Your rays.
And as much as I must still reflect
You will give me.
But as much as I cannot take up
You will have already assigned to others."[28]

—Alexander Solzhenitsyn, *A
Pictorial Autobiography*

3

Confession

Abyss or Bridge?

"To confess your sins to God is not to tell him anything he doesn't already know. Until you confess them, however, they are the abyss between you. When you confess them, they become the bridge."[1]

—Frederick Buechner, *Wishful Thinking, A Theological ABC*

The Acknowledgement . . .

"The fundamental prayer of confession . . . is the acknowledgement that we are separated from God, and cannot overcome that separation by ourselves."[2]

—John B. Coburn, *Prayer and Personal Religion*

Letting in the Light

"The prayer of honest confession before the loving reality

27

of God and his truth is like opening the door into a dark, stale room and letting in the light and fresh air. Once the door is open, you wonder why you remained in the darkness so long."³

—Lance Webb, *The Art of Personal Prayer*

A Strange Necessity

"There is a strange necessity in the human spirit that a man deal with his sin before God. This necessity is honored in prayer when the deed is laid bare and the guilt acknowledged. I do not know how it happens or quite how to describe it, but I do know that again and again man has come away from prayer freed of his guilt, and with his sin forgiven; he then has a sense of being totally understood, completely dealt with, thoroughly experienced, and utterly healed."⁴

—Howard Thurman, *Disciplines of the Spirit*

The Dark Spots of Life

"Fugitive islands of secret reservations elude us. Rationalizations hide them. Intending absolute honesty, we can only bring ourselves steadfastly into His presence and pray, 'Cleanse thou me from secret faults.' And in the X-ray light of Eternity we may be given to see the dark spots of life, and divine grace may be given to reinforce our will to complete abandonment in Him. For the guidance of the Light is critical, acid, sharper than a two-edged sword. He asks all, but He gives all."⁵

—Thomas R. Kelly, *A Testament of Devotion*

As Much As We Can Bear

"We stop the life of concealment, of pretending that

no one knows or need know. We say that we are living in the light, we are content to have it so, only more so, we want to be wholly in the light if possible. It is not wholly possible subjectively, because we cannot bear the whole truth, but confession is the desire for as much as we can bear."[6]

—J. Neville Ward, *The Use of Praying*

Unworthiness and Contrition

"Confession . . . has two levels. First comes acknowledgement of unworthiness and therefore of need. . . . Consciousness of need is not enough. It leads inevitably to the sincere sorrow and repentance which the medieval thinkers called 'contrition,' distinguishing it carefully from 'attrition,' which is a state of mind induced by fear of punishment."[7]

—Roger Hazelton, *The Root and Flower of Prayer*

God Was with Us

"When we confess our sins we are not telling God anything he does not know. He was with us and obscurely in us when we were doing the sins we are confessing."[8]

—J. Neville Ward, *The Use of Praying*

New Beginnings

"Make every day a day of new beginnings and of fresh consecration to the service of God. Having sought and found God's forgiveness for the wrongs of the past, turn your back resolutely on these failures and face the new life which, by the grace of God, is opening up before you."[9]

—John S. Bonnell, *Psychology for Pastor and People*

In Forgiving Hands

". . . we confess our bankruptcy; and if anyone is unwilling to do so, he must give up asking God's forgiveness. We must recognize that our own cause is lost, and if we do, it becomes for us a victorious cause, for it is then in the hands of Him who has forgiven and who still forgives."[10]

—Karl Barth, *Prayer According to the Catechisms of the Reformation*

To Lance the Wound

"In surgical compassion *prayer lances the infected wound which our self-will has sealed.* How? By confession. . . . To confess to wise human ears and to God's ears, making full acknowledgment, is to lance the wound. Prayer is thus the beginning of healing."[11]

—George A. Buttrick, *Prayer*

So Long Prayed Against

"No evil habit is so ingrained nor so long prayed against (as it seemed) in vain, that it cannot, even in dry old age, be whisked away."[12]

—C. S. Lewis, *Letters to Malcolm: Chiefly on Prayer*

Deeply Tranquil and Joyful

". . . our meditation should begin with the realization of our nothingness and helplessness in the presence of God. This need not be a mournful or discouraging experience. On the contrary, it can be deeply tranquil and joyful since it brings us in direct contact with the source of all joy and all life."[13]

—Thomas Merton, *The Climate of Monastic Prayer*

Stained and Soiled

"This daily prayer for forgiveness represents the washing of the hands and feet of the wayfarer which have been stained and soiled by the mud and dust of the journey."[14]

—C. F. Andrews, *Christ and Prayer*

Solemnity Is Ridiculous

"The life of prayer outside the strength of Christ is often a solemn, anxious, heavy striving, where a person feels it is all up to him whether or not he reaches the ineffable Light, and if he fails, he fails. But solemnity is ridiculous in the Christian. He has learned already that he will fail if he stands by himself. That is why he is standing in Christ. That is why Christ came into the world. The Christian has no need to defend himself to his conscience. He can laugh while growing."[15]

—Flora Wuellner, *Prayer and the Living Christ*

Forgiveness and Prayer

"We cannot pray until we are forgiven; and we cannot know ourselves to be forgiven until we pray."[16]

—John Casteel, *The Promise of Prayer*

Rigid Ego-Made Prisons

"Confessional prayer is the continuous opening of our small selves to the influence of God in the faith that He will dissolve these rigid ego-made prisons, these 'caves of illusion' and brings us, as St. Paul says, into 'the glorious liberty of His own sons.'"[17]

—John B. Magee, *Reality and Prayer*

Still in Grey Weather

"Is there not something un-Christian in rising from confession still in grey weather, and without the sunshine having broken through?"[18]

—Arthur Gossip, *In the Secret Place of the Most High*

Free, Full Forgiveness

"To look upon sinning men, seeing their obvious impenitence, sensing the hideous twist in their natures, recognising their weakness and brokenness of will, knowing the detestable tendency of mean human nature to mistake gentleness for weakness and make mercy an excuse for sin—to discern all this, and *still* to assure them of God's free, full forgiveness, trusting both Him and them where appearances are dead against such trust, is the great Christian adventure."[19]

—E. Herman, *Creative Prayer*

Impassable Barriers

"The harboring of a grudge, the subtle wish for another's harm, the envy that corrupts the heart, even if it finds no expression in word or deed—such attitudes always prove impassable barriers to spontaneous prayer."[20]

—Harry Emerson Fosdick, *The Meaning of Prayer*

Gifts of Shame and Guilt

"We do not ask for shame and guilt but, on the contrary, have every reason not to want these gifts. Yet Christ gives them to us without our asking. He knows we need them, and therefore he gives them to us.

"We should rejoice that we are able to experience shame and guilt in his presence, for by that we know we are sensitive to his holy life and can respond. . . . Then we shall know the peace of acceptance and forgiveness, not the morbidity of brooding."[21]

—Charles Whiston, *Pray, a Study of Distinctively Christian Praying*

Crying from the Depths

"Confession is more than wiping away life's little wrongs with the once-over of a hasty prayer: 'I'm sorry, God.' Confession is crying from the depths. It is probing my fundamental character as a human being and discovering that the core of my personal existence is out of alignment with the truth."[22]

—Thomas Troeger, *Rage! Reflect. Rejoice!*

A Door Open Towards Our Sin

"We may confess and seek pardon from God and keep a door open towards our sin. That is not enough for real contrition. There is . . . cause to fear the confession which does not involve a sincere purpose, and does not expect any fullness of answer to the cry for help which is at the heart of real confession."[23]

—George S. Stewart, *The Lower Levels of Prayer*

Confession Fails Unless . . .

"When confession becomes the dominant mood in prayer, and sins and sorrows are endlessly disinterred, prayer becomes morbidly unsound. Prayer should usually be composed in a major key. It should dwell in light, not in shadow. Confession fails unless in the very confession it turns to a prayer of resolve and faith. . . . God does not wish us to remember what He is willing to forget. Yet confession is an essential mood in prayer. Possibly no mood has more instant blessing."[24]

—George A. Buttrick, *Prayer*

Our Helplessness

"Our former self-conceit and self-sufficiency reassert themselves. The result is that we fail again to grasp the meaning of helplessness. Once more it fills us with anxiety and perplexity. Everything becomes snarled again. We are not certain of the forgiveness of sins. . . . Then our helplessness re-establishes us in our right relationship both to God and to man. Above all it restores us to the right attitude in prayer."[25]

—O. Hallesby, *Prayer*

Spiritual Fatigue

"Honest, rigorous self-examination with the stripping off of rationalizations and alibis is required. Bending backward and straining to lift the weight of one's sin out of an imagined cesspool of iniquity is not! By this procedure one incurs spiritual fatigue but seldom finds rest in God."[26]

—Georgia Harkness, *Prayer and the Common Life*

Made Whole Again

"Forgiveness is the answer to the child's dream of a miracle by which what is broken is made whole again, what is soiled is again made clean. The dream explains why we need to be forgiven, and why we must forgive. In the presence of God, nothing stands between Him and us—we *are* forgiven. But we *cannot* feel His presence if anything is allowed to stand between ourselves and others."[27]

—Dag Hammarskjöld, *Markings*

Before Sleep

"A well-ordered life, as a Christian, will instinctively employ the last moments before sleep for confession of sin and for realizing anew the peace of God's forgiveness."[28]

> —C. F. Andrews, *Christ and Prayer*

Reconciliation Be Made

"It is a decisive rule of every Christian fellowship that every dissension that the day has brought must be healed in the evening. It is perilous for the Christian to lie down to sleep with an unreconciled heart. Therefore, it is well that there be a special place for the prayer of brotherly forgiveness in every evening's devotion, that reconciliation be made and fellowship established anew."[29]

> —Dietrich Bonhoeffer, *Life Together*

Acts of Restitution

"The acceptance of God's forgiving mercy must be followed by appropriate acts of restitution. The willingnesss to rebuild what our past acts and attitudes have destroyed may be the acid test of the whole experience of forgiveness. Such restitution will not win forgiveness—that is given without price—but it may mark the acceptance of mercy with the sign of authenticity."[30]

> —John B. Magee, *Reality and Prayer*

I Can Breathe Again

"Prayer is renewing the sense of God's forgiveness. It is heightening my interior awareness of divine pardon. It is letting God lift the coffin lid of guilt so I can breathe again."[31]

> —Thomas Troeger, *Rage! Reflect. Rejoice!*

4

Thanksgiving

First and Most

"When I go to God I want to thank Him, first and most, for the kindness that remembers me even when I forget Him . . . ."[1]

—Arthur Gossip, *In the Secret Place of the Most High*

Begin Each Day

"In our daily practice of prayer we should begin each day with an act of loving thankfulness to God. . . .[2]

—C. F. Andrews, *Christ and Prayer*

Your Inalienable Right

"Thank God for the opportunity of communing with Him, and for the people who have asked you to pray, and for the occasion—yes, even for the troubles that made it incumbent on you to seek Him. Be thankful for every experience which helps you to grow spiritually. Rejoice in your inalienable right to come to Him in prayer."[3]

—Kermit Olsen, *First Steps in Prayer*

Learn to Give Thanks

"A Christian has to learn how to give thanks and indeed to learn it again and again."[4]

—Ladislaus Boros, *Christian Prayer*

The First Thing You Do

"Awake in the morning and the first thing you do, thank God for it, even if you don't feel particularly happy about the day which is to come. 'This day which the Lord has made, let us rejoice and be grateful in it.'"[5]

—Anthony Bloom, *Beginning to Pray*

The Given Condition

"Every man who knows God must return thanks to him. He recognizes what God is, what God has done for him in Jesus Christ; he enters into the condition that has been given us in Jesus Christ. And in this condition man prays."[6]

—Karl Barth, *Prayer According to the Catechisms of the Reformation*

It Is Your Nature

"Praise means a 'breaking out' in spontaneous sound. To

ask why men should feel thankful in face of earth and sky, and should 'break out' in prayers of gratitude, is like asking why birds should sing: it is their nature. Birds cannot—and men should not—deny their nature."[7]

—George Buttrick, *Prayer*

Grateful . . . Secure . . . Joyful

"We must know how to say, 'Thank you.' Our days are filled with the gifts the Lord showers on us. If we were in the habit of taking stock of them, at night we should be like a 'queen for a day,' dazzled and happy with so many blessings. We should then be grateful to God, secure because he gives us everything, joyful because we know that every day he will renew his gifts."[8]

—Michel Quoist, *Prayers*

Thanks for the Opportunity

"God doesn't want us to sit down to turkey dinner at Thanksgiving, or to any meal, and choke on it. But He does want us to see that it can't be 'dinner as usual.' There are brothers and sisters of ours who are equally blessed (loved) by God, who do not show signs of being 'blessed' with health, food, justice, housing, clothing, jobs. They are God's message to us that the goods of His creation need to be equitably shared. They are God's invitation to us, to understand that we are called to give thanks for the opportunity of changing the world."[9]

—William Toohey, *Life After Birth, Spirituality for College Students*

Meaningful and Holy

"It is a Christian conviction that life in itself is neither meaningful nor holy, but that it can be made meaningful and holy. Thankfulness consecrates it, makes it meaningful and holy."[10]

—J. Neville Ward, *The Use of Praying*

Good for Us

"To be able to express our gratitude is a rewarding, satisfying kind of emotion. . . . We know that God has no need for our thanks because he is full and complete in and of himself, but he knows it is good for *us* and that should be enough."[11]

—Orien Johnson, *Becoming Transformed*

Grateful Surprise

". . . each of us has known grateful surprise for a dream come true, a further range of life opened up by new love or friendship, or a sudden flashing moment when 'joy comes forth from sorrow, and light from terrors past.'"[12]

—Roger Hazelton, *The Root and Flowers of Prayer*

Temporal and Spiritual Gifts

"If you are as ungrateful as I often am, my friend, I would pass this advice on to you: begin by giving thanks to God for the temporal gifts you have received from Him, such as physical health, the use of your mental faculties, strength for your daily tasks, the desire to work, house and home, food and clothing and the dear ones whom you love and who love you. Begin with these things and you will notice that it will become easier for you to see and to give thanks for the spiritual gifts which the Lord has showered upon you."[13]

—O. Hallesby, *Prayer*

Praise

"The single most remarkable trait of Black prayers was the total absence of the spirit of hate, revenge, and malice, especially to the White power structure. There was a positive affirmation of life, expressed in praise. This tradition was filled with utterances of 'Thank you, Jesus,' 'Yes, Lord,' and 'Through it all, the Lord has been good to me.'"[14]

—Harold Carter, *The Prayer Tradition of Black People*

Just to Give Thanks

"But is it not like God, in His compassion, that we, who can do so little for Him, are accounted by Him to have wrought Him signal service if, with sincere and grateful hearts, we remember to give thanks, just to give thanks for all He is, and all that He has done, and all that He has given?"[15]

—Arthur Gossip, *In the Secret Place of the Most High*

For Ever Blessing

"We well know that the divine mercy outran our best memory, yet we should be for ever blessing the Lord."[16]

—W. Graham Scroggie, *Method in Prayer*

Happy in God

"To be a Christian is to be happy in God, and whether or not we can sing with our lips, we ought with grateful hearts to render to him our tribute of thanksgiving for our very existence."[17]

—Georgia Harkness, *Prayer and the Common Life*

Thoughtlessness and Carelessness

"Perhaps the greatest of all hindrances to our abounding in thanksgiving is simple thoughtlessness and carelessness. We are so preoccupied with the rush of things that crowd upon us that we forget to be grateful to God."[18]

—Albert Wieand, *The Gospel of Prayer*

One Yes to God

"We are all bound in some way. None of us is absolutely free to move or quite flexible in the hands of God. Therefore we should all say to him: Lord, do not pass by until I have noticed your arrival. Lord, do not stop knocking at my door, beating and pushing against me, until I have opened up to you. Such is the stillness of the man who is ready and willing. The whole essence of that stillness is to be one Yes to God."[19]

—Ladislaus Boros, *"Prerequisites for Christian Prayer"*

What God Has Done

"It has always seemed odd to me that whereas we are ready to examine ourselves for what we have done or are, we almost never think of examining our lives to see what God has done in them and for us. If we did so, we should find that thanksgiving would be natural and inevitable."[20]

—Norman Pittenger, *Praying Today, Practical Thoughts on Prayer*

Our Inclination

"The older we get, the greater becomes our inclination to give thanks, especially heavenwards. We feel more strongly than we could possibly have ever felt before that life is a free gift, and receive every unqualifiedly good hour in gratefully reaching out hands, as an unexpected gift."[21]

> —Martin Buber, *The Way of Response*

Countless Acts of Kindness

"It really looks as if God has lavished upon me his most tender and motherly care; he has led me out of so many difficulties, and through countless acts of kindness he has brought me here to Rome. It must be for some particular purpose of his: there can be no other reason for my Master's infinite generosity."[22]

> —Pope John XXIII, *Journal of a Soul*

Taking Things for Granted

"Thanksgiving means thanking God for all the good gifts which he has given to us. One of the great dangers of life is that we should take things for granted just because they come to us regularly and every day."[23]

> —William Barclay, *Prayers for Young People*

The Other Face of Faith

"It is indeed good to give thanks to the Lord. For thanksgiving is the other face of faith. You can't have one without the other."[24]

> —Louis Cassels, *Haircuts and Holiness*

Thanksgiving for Freedom

"We make of our silence a paean of thanksgiving for Freedom. We make an offering of quiet gratitude to God for those men and women who in the darkness of an age lighted candles, first in their hearts, then in their families, then in the common way, that darkness might not triumph over the spirit of men."[25]

—Howard Thurman, *The Centering Moment*

Returned to God
"The offering of gratitude is not complete until we have returned to God the total life which he has created, preserved, blessed, and redeemed."[26]

—John Casteel, *The Promise of Prayer*

The Final Word
"That word of thanksgiving is a word we shall finally be able to speak only when we and the whole creation are gathered together in offering to the creator, but it is also a word which, in a tentative and partial way, we are able to speak now in the anticipation and hope of being able to speak it finally."[27]

—James E. Griffiss, *A Silent Path to God*

The Language of Heaven
"Praise is the language of heaven. And we had better start to learn it here."[28]

—Arthur Gossip, *In the Secret Place of the Most High*

Backward-Looking Prayer
"It is more important to thank God for blessings received than to pray for them beforehand. For that forward-looking

prayer, though right as an expression of dependence upon God, is still self-centered in part, at least, of its interest; there is something which we hope to gain by our prayer. But the backward-looking act of thanksgiving is quite free from this. In itself it is quite selfless. Thus it is akin to love."[29]

—William Temple, *Daily Readings from Willliam Temple*

Never . . . an End

"We shall never come to an end of thanksgiving, for God's blessings are the outpourings of infinite, eternal love."[30]

—George S. Stewart, *The Lower
Levels of Prayer*

Petition

Acknowledgement of Lordship

"The simple and direct act of petition must always be at the center of prayer, because it is an acknowledgement that God is the Lord of all life."[1]

—James E. Griffiss, *A Silent Path to God*

The Courage to Pray

"Many people today no longer pray even in private. Prayer seems strange, alienating and inaccessible. We feel no inclination for it even when prayer is the only form of language that can express our lives and feelings adequately. Surely no Christian nowadays would dispute that we need the courage to pray, especially for ourselves."[2]

—Johann Metz, *The Courage to Pray*

Longing to Give

"Petitionary prayer is no more begging God to help us than the branch is begging the vine for the life stream. To be sure the branch is absolutely dependent. Its life and growth come from the vine. But the vine's nature is to give. It 'longs' to give. So with God through Christ. It is God's eternal nature to give."[3]

—Flora Wuellner, *Prayer and the Living Christ*

The Safeguard

"Petitionary prayer, because it is often a very wrestling with God, is the safeguard of other prayer moods. For instance, mystic communion without the forthrightness and practicality of petition, might become by 'absorption into the Infinite' both an escape from the demands of earth and a surrender of the birthright of personality."[4]

—George A. Buttrick, *Prayer*

A Prayer of Asking

"When the disciples asked Jesus to teach them to pray, he did not respond by advising them to meditate on the good nor did he teach them sophisticated techniques of contemplation. He told them to ask, to seek, to knock; and the model prayer that he taught them is one that consists of a series of petitions. It is quite unmistakably a prayer of asking."[5]

—John Macquarrie, *The Humility of God*

Conquest, Not Evasion

"What prayer does is to enable us, not to find a way round the hard thing, but to go straight through it, not to avoid it but to accept it and overcome it. Prayer is not evasion; prayer is conquest."[6]

—William Barclay, *A Spiritual Autobiography*

God's Answer

"I believe we often do get God's answer almost the instant we ask for it, *but we don't like God's answer,* and so we persist in asking, hoping that God will answer otherwise."[7]

—Frank Laubach, *Channels of Spiritual Power*

God or His Adversary

". . . all of us are in a sense praying all the time, in our ambitions, our basic longings, and our vital principles. We are always focused either on God or on his adversary."[8]

—Douglas Steere, *Dimensions of Prayer*

Available for Our Guidance

"Because of our own ignorance, our helplessness and impatience, because of the spiritual hindrances without and within, with which only prayer can cope, because God knows what we cannot know and makes his knowledge available for our guidance, we ought to seek the habit of discernment of duty through prayer."[9]

—Robert Speer, *A Christian's Habits*

Calm

"A doctor who sees a patient give himself to prayer, can indeed rejoice. The calm engendered by prayer is a powerful aid to healing."[10]

—Alexis Carrel, *Prayer*

A Door Opens

". . . is it not the attested fact of all Christian experience that when we pray a door opens, and we are face to face with One wiser than our wisest and better than our best?"[11]

—Henry Sloane Coffin, *Joy in Believing, Selections of Henry Sloane Coffin*

Contact with Christ

"Keep close to the New Testament Christ, and then ask for anything you desire in that contact."[12]

—P. T. Forsyth, *The Soul of Prayer*

So Often Refused

". . . I'm not asking why our petitions are so often refused. Anyone can see in general that this must be so. In our ignorance we ask what is not good for us or for others, or not even intrinsically possible."[13]

—C. S. Lewis, *Letters to Malcolm: Chiefly on Prayer*

The Fundamental Pattern

"The fundamental pattern of petition is the conscious offering of our needs and desires to God, allowing Him to purify and mature them, and then trusting Him totally with the results."[14]

—John B. Magee, *Reality and Prayer*

Mundane Prayers

"Do not be ashamed to offer 'selfish' prayers, or to seek

God's help in 'little' things. Jesus included in his model prayer a petition for bread, which is about as mundane a request as you can make."[15]

—Louis Cassels, *Haircuts and Holiness*

Answer the Man

"Even when God cannot answer affirmatively the man's petition, he can answer the man."[16]

—Harry Emerson Fosdick, *The Meaning of Prayer*

Anxiety and Expectancy

"Eagerness, the response proper to petition, is compounded of anxiety and expectancy. . . . His anxiety that the dark tangled places of his life should be lighted by the ways of God, that he may somehow appropriate God's favor to himself, is tempered by the waiting, wondering expectancy of a creaturely dependence."[17]

—Roger Hazelton, *The Root and Flower of Prayer*

A New Situation

"Prayer always creates a new situation."[18]

—George S. Stewart, *The Lower Levels of Prayer*

Let God Decide

". . . even though you have misused prayer often, continue nevertheless to make known your desires to God in all things. It is when we can speak with one another about anything and everything that conversation really affords us freedom and relief. Let Him decide whether you are to receive what you ask for or not."[19]

—O. Hallesby, *Prayer*

Wisdom and Strength

"It is in the petition for moral and spiritual help that most of our praying ought to center. What is sometimes referred to as the 'gimme' prayer will recede into the background if it is replaced by the petition that God will give us the wisdom and strength to meet his high demands."[20]

—Georgia Harkness, *Prayer and the Common Life*

Heartfelt Supplication

"The essence of true prayer is heartfelt supplication, bringing before God one's innermost needs and requests in the confident expectation that God will hear and answer."[21]

—Donald G. Bloesch, *The Struggle of Prayer*

Amen!

"In the Lord's Prayer there are seven petitions while adoration and confession and thanksgiving and submission are there mainly by implication. And even they are to give introduction to and build a foundation for full assurance of faith that the petitions will be granted. And they lead onto the 'Amen!' which means in essence, 'Certainly it will be so!'"[22]

—Albert Wieand, *The Gospel of Prayer*

Magic or Religion?

"Several anthropologists, studying the difference between magic and religion in primitive peoples, have indicated that the latter (religion) is much more an intended conformity of things human with the divine, whereas the former (magic) is the effort, by use of formulae or rites, to bring the divine into conformity with things human. Unhappily, a good deal of petitionary prayer as well as intercession seems to be based on the 'magical' premise rather than the 'religious' one."[23]

> —Norman Pittenger, *Praying Today*

God's Adorable Providence

"We should be spurred on to ask God again and again, since the Christian prayer of petition contains an inspiring truth. It is a trustful recognition of God's adorable providence. As soon as this truth is grasped, all sense of disappointment in God's apparent failure to listen to us when we ask will disappear. Our most urgent and profound request is, after all, not to be helped to achieve some individual aim. It is to be given the grace to enable us to be inwardly transformed so that we shall be able to see the true meaning of life with new eyes."[24]

> —Ladislaus Boros, *Christian Prayer*

In All Their Paltriness

"Religious contemplation and worship must not become an ethereal domain of solitary and timeless reflection, insulated from the burdens of daily existence. Hence the supreme importance of including our personal needs, in all their paltriness, within the perspective of our yearning to become part of His design. It is not as a disembodied soul that man stands in prayer, but as a living human being, with needs and responsibilities."[25]

> —Jacob Agus, *"The Meaning of Prayer"*

An Answer
"An honest little girl who prayed each night was asked if God had given her an answer to what she had asked him, and her instant reply was, 'Yes, he said "No".'"[26]

—Douglas Steere, *Dimensions of Prayer*

Waging War on One's Knees
"No one in modern times has lifted the dimension of facing life on one's knees as has the late Dr. Martin Luther King, Jr. When he called on his followers to face their enemies with a prayer and nonviolence based on Christian love, he was speaking to a people whose history made them receptive to this message. Waging war on one's knees was not new! Dr. King simply gave it a new dimension."[27]

—Harold Carter, *The Prayer Tradition of Black People*

Consent to Take Them
"Often God cannot give us the things we need until we are prepared to consent to take them; and petition means asking God to give us the things which he knows we need, and telling him that we are ready now to take them."[28]

—William Barclay, *Prayers for Young People*

How Can I Take?
"It might help us to remember that if God were not willing to give, then we could wrest nothing out of his hands. But if he is willing to give, then we have only to take. The Bible says he is more willing to give than we are to ask. How *can* I take? I take by affirming that his love and peace and power are at my disposal and that his peace is flooding my heart, even while I bow in this inner room."[29]

—Leslie Weatherhead, *A Private House of Prayer*

Some . . . Are Answered

Some petitions are not answered, and if they were we could not worship Him, for His ways are higher than our ways. But some petitions are answered: He is surprise of Mercy, outgoing Gladness, Rescue, Healing, and Life."[30]

—George A. Buttrick, *Prayer*

Do We Want the Answer?

"As we pray for increase of strength or virtue, let us remember that the answer is likely to take the form of opportunity to exercise it, like the lady who prayed for patience and was provided with an ill-tempered cook."[31]

—William Temple, *Daily Readings from William Temple*

6

Intercession

Its Advantages

"Intercession smooths the rough edges of Christian sympathy, corrects its nearsightedness, expands its range of vision, breaks down its walls of smugness. These are its advantages."[1]

—Roger Hazelton, *The Root and Flower of Prayer*

Pointing to Them

"When Jane Addams went to confront the alderman of Chicago with the conditions of the area in which Hull House stood, she would take with her one of the mothers from the neighborhood to remind her why she had come to confront these officials. Our prayers become an act of taking into the presence of God with us the persons, peoples, causes, concerns that we are to pray for, and we bring them before him, pointing to them as we look at him, and wait for him to do with and for them his 'good pleasure.'"[2]

—John Casteel, *The Promise of Prayer*

Sharing God's Creative Power

"God set up the universe in such a way that we can influence it not only by the exercise of human intelligence but also by the exercise of human prayer. God has made us more than spectators to his creative power; we also share in it."[3]

—Mark Link, *Breakaway*

The Mystery of God

"The Lord could do without our intercession and our praise. Yet it is the mystery of God that he should require us, his co-workers, to keep on praying and never lose heart."[4]

—Roger Schutz, *The Rule of Taizé*

A Live Wire

"A real man or woman of prayer . . . should be a live wire, a link between God's grace and the world that needs it. In so far as you have given your lives to God, you have offered yourselves, without conditions, as transmitters of His saving and enabling love; and the will and love, the emotional drive, which you thus consecrate to God's purposes, can do actual work on supernatural levels for those for whom you are called upon to pray."[5]

—Evelyn Underhill, *The Evelyn Underhill Reader*

In the Largest and Deepest Way

"When we try to intercede, in the largest and deepest way possible, it is an inspiration to know that we are joining in prayer not only with our fellow-Christians but with many people outside the visible church."[6]

—Olive Wyon, *Prayer*

Concern for Others

"The man who shares his concern for others with God in prayer does two things at the same time. He exposes the need of the other person to his total life and resources, making it possible for new insights of helpfulness and creativity to emerge in him. In other words he sees more clearly how to relate himself to the other person's need. In the second place, he may quicken the spirit of his friend to a sudden upsurging of the hunger for God, with the result that he is in the way of help from the vast creative energies of God."[7]

—Howard Thurman, *Disciplines of the Spirit*

A Vicarious Exercise

"Prayer at its highest reach climbs up to a vicarious exercise of the soul. I mean by that somewhat abused word, 'vicarious,' that we can, and do, lend our souls out as organs of love and suffering in fellowship-prayer for others who are in need of help and comfort."[8]

—Rufus M. Jones, *Rufus Jones Speaks to Our Time, An Anthology*

That Means Me!

"Very often, when I used to take services, in the prayer of intercession I would pray for 'those whose task it is to keep clean and sweet this place of worship'. And again and again I would find a church officer or a church cleaner would come to say thanks that they had been remembered in prayer—a remembrance which seldom happened. At least once in a while every person in the congregation should be able to say of something in a service: 'That means me!'"[9]

—William Barclay, *A Spiritual Autobiography*

Pray for Enemies

"Put up your guns; throw away your bricks and bottles; put away your knives. We cannot allow ourselves to fall so low as to adopt the methods of our oppressors. Let us go home and pray for those who hate us, knowing God will see us through."[10]

—Martin Luther King, Jr., quoted in *The Prayer Tradition of Black People*

Vast World Needs

"Our hands are so tiny; and the world's needs are so vast, that we are forced back upon God, who alone is sufficient."[11]

—Arthur Gossip, *In the Secret Place of the Most High*

Channels of Cooperation

"Our prayer when it is at its best restores and strengthens the relationship between us and God and in some indescribable way between God and the ones we pray for. We accept the miracle of radio and TV receiving sets which fulfill the conditions so that words and music and happenings in one place are sent to all parts of the world. Surely on the higher level of spiritual realities, the mind and heart of a loving God has provided for us channels of cooperation which when used, may bring to us and our human loved ones the presence of a new and greater life than we yet know."[12]

—Lance Webb, *The Art of Personal Prayer*

Loving Thoughts for Others

"It is not the single act of prayer that is needed so much as the prayer life. All our loving thoughts for others, made one with the Divine Love, are real prayers."[13]

—C. F. Andrews, *Christ and Prayer*

Names That "Spring Out"

"How do we know who to pray for? A nun who spends much of her day in intercessory prayer described to me how, out of the long list of people in various kinds of extreme trouble for whom she was asked to pray, one or two names would 'spring out' at her, and she would know that they were the ones who specially needed attention in prayer. When the mind is in a certain state of quietness and attention it can become aware in this sort of way, as it can also become aware of the necessity for certain sorts of action, the purpose of which it may not understand at the time—for example, going to see someone for no obvious reason."[14]

—Monica Furlong, *Contemplating Now*

Spiritual Blood Donation

"Intercessory praying may be called spiritual blood donation. Intercession is the giving of self to Christ, the giving of life, love, and energy to enter the lives of others through him for their blessing. We give to them not directly but through Jesus Christ. Direct giving might often be harmful; but intercession through Jesus Christ always benefits the other."[15]

—Charles Whiston, *Pray, A Study of Distinctively Christian Praying*

A Wingless Bird

"Faith is expressed in prayer. I am always astonished at the number of convinced Christians who, through shyness or false shame, do not dare to pray with their parents, their friends, or even with those who ask for their religious help. Their ministry is like a wingless bird."[16]

—Paul Tournier, *The Person Reborn*

People to Be Prayed For
"The increasing list of people to be prayed for is . . . one of the burdens of old age. I have a scruple about crossing anyone off the list. When I say a scruple, I mean precisely a scruple. I don't really think that if one prays for a man at all it is a duty to pray for him all my life. But when it comes to dropping him *now*, this particular day, it somehow goes against the grain."[17]

—C. S. Lewis, *Letters to Malcolm: Chiefly on Prayer*

A Vital Necessity
"Knowing all human life to be one; knowing ourselves to be vitally and indissolubly knit to our brethren in God; knowing that He sees mankind as living in relations of mutual interdependence, united by their common response to eternal love, intercession becomes a vital necessity."[18]

—E. Herman, *Creative Prayer*

Open the Pipeline at Both Ends
"[The] prayer of intercession connects God and other people: it is one of the purest forms of service, the mightiest single power on earth. When we pray for others we open the pipeline at both ends, and God flows through to bless those for whom we pray."[19]

—Frank Laubach, *Channels of Spiritual Power*

Lightning Conductors
"As Christians, we believe that the great intercessory prayer for healing and renewing is eternally flowing from Christ the Son to the Source of all being—the Father, and that the loving response forever flows through Christ to the created world. Christians by praying link themsleves to that power

which is Christ's prayer. We are opening ourselves to its radiance and its force. We are becoming like lightning conductors to channelize this loving power to the person for whom we pray."[20]

—Flora Wuellner, *Prayer and the Living Christ*

Occasional Eddies

"*The chief obstacles to intercession are moral.* We live for what we can get; our dominant desires are selfish. The main current of us runs in the channel of our mean ambitions, and our thoughts of other people and of great causes are but occasional eddies on the surface of the stream."[21]

—Harry Emerson Fosdick, *The Meaning of Prayer*

God's Glorious Purpose

"We begin our prayer with a weight of anxiety on our mind, that finds no relief in active work, or in the dull mechanical exercise of routine and habit; but if along with our Master and Teacher in the School of Prayer we can rise to the height of the vision of God's glorious purpose in the world and the fulfillment of His will for all mankind, then it often happens that our tiny troubles—however large they may appear to us—get back their true proportion, and we are able to lose them in the vast amplitude of the love of God."[22]

—C. F. Andrews, *Christ and Prayer*

Whatever the Outcome

"What is important is not to decide in each case just how much effect prayer had, for lacking divine wisdom we cannot estimate the delicate balance of forces involved. What is vital is to live so grounded in prayer that, whatever the outcome, we will still go on trusting God and praying for spiritual victory for ourselves and others."[23]

—Georgia Harkness, *Prayer and the Common Life*

Giving Back Our Personal Energy

"Intercessory prayer . . . may be actually the giving back to God of our personal energy that He may use it to strengthen and help and bless another soul."[24]

—Albert Belden, *The Practice of Prayer*

And Who Knows?

"It's so easy to promise to pray for people, or just plan to pray for people, and forget. So many afflictions, so many tragedies or desperate hopes that cry out for intercession. Only an instant of my time, only a few words, a thought—and who knows? It may be the only word of prayer that person will get. . . . Or my prayer will join the chorus of other prayers that often work such miracles."[25]

—Marjorie Holmes, *How Can I Find You, God?*

The Whole World

"Intercession is, perhaps, the most expansive element in prayer on its more active side, for every field of interest which it annexes opens out to view other and wider fields to be entered and possessed, until the whole world is brought within its province."[26]

—W. Graham Scroggie, *Method in Prayer*

The Glow of All Saints

"Each saint has something to give which adds to the glow of all saints; and only by self-loss in that one radiance can make his own life complete."[27]

—Evelyn Underhill, *The Evelyn Underhill Reader*

Become Part of the Answer

" . . . especially in intercessory prayer, we ought never to decide that we have done all that was necessary when we have prayed. This seems a particular serious temptation and one to be avoided at all costs. Whenever one prays, one should become part of the answer of the prayer. . . . The prayer itself ought to make us more responsible and aware of the needs of others and thereby increase our own personal responses to persons for whom we pray."[28]

—H. Wayne Pipkin, *Christian Meditation, Its Art and Practice*

An Opening

"If even a small number of people are interceding before God, we may say that a way is being provided into that dense texture of human relationships in which we are all bound up. An opening has been made so that the divine will can have access. And since God's will is for peace and health and wholeness, prayer can be a dynamic transforming force. . . ."[29]

—John Macquarrie, *The Humility of God*

For All Living Creatures

"It was quite incomprehensible to me—this was before I began going to school—why in my evening prayers I should pray for human beings only. So when my mother had prayed with me and had kissed me good night, I used to add silently a prayer that I had composed myself for all living creatures. It ran thus: 'O, heavenly Father, protect and bless all things that have breath; guard them from all evil, and let them sleep in peace.'"[30]

—Albert Schweitzer, *Memoirs of Childhood and Youth*

7

Silence

The Most Wonderful Thing
"The best and most wonderful thing that can happen to you in this life, is that you should be silent and let God work and speak."[1]

—Dag Hammarskjöld, *Markings*

A Stillness of Soul
"If we put aside pressing cares and allow the life of the universe to whisper to our hearts, living becomes pure joy. Then the heart will be detached from illusions and worldly cares be overcome. Even in the midst of the most chaotic scenes there will be a stillness of soul which is undisturbable."[2]

—Kagawa, *Kagawa*

The Softer Light
"Prayer is turning our three-way lamp down to 60 watts

and laying aside the newspaper and being satisfied with the softer light and God's presence in the silence of the moment."[3]

—Thomas Troeger, *Rage! Reflect. Rejoice!*

Not a Noisy Process

"Creativity usually springs from quietness. We cannot hear a tree grow, yet the power of God is at work there. The growth of a spirit is not a noisy process, but it can be fostered by the preparation of a self that knows how to listen and is ready and willing to do it."[4]

—Edgar N. Jackson, *Understanding Prayer*

Total Stability

"If you are silent, you can rest in the 'eye' of the cyclone or the hurricane, in the calm there, but leaving the storm around you to rage, while you are where God is, at the only point of total stability. But this point of total stability is not a point when nothing happens. It is the point where all the conflicting tensions meet and are counterbalanced by one another and are held in the powerful hand of God."[5]

—Anthony Bloom, *Beginning to Pray*

Making Some Desert

". . . if you cannot go into the desert, you must nonetheless 'make some desert' in your life. Every now and then leaving men and looking for solitude to restore, in prolonged silence and prayer, the stuff of your soul. This is the meaning of 'desert' in your spiritual life."[6]

—Carlo Carretto, *Letters from the Desert*

Great Stillness

"Geologists tell us that there are certain crystals that can only come to their perfect form through a season of great stillness. Similarly it is quite certain that periods of such absolute rest in God are essential to the perfect spiritual and moral health of the soul."[7]

—Albert Belden, *The Practice of Prayer*

The Silences of Your Heart

"Hasten unto Him who calls you in the silences of your heart. The Hound of Heaven is ever near us, the voice of the Shepherd is calling us home."[8]

—Thomas R. Kelly, *A Testament of Devotion*

Silentiotherapy

"Some silences are painful, burdened with unease, reticence, and dissembled thoughts. Some are distant, cold, absent silences. But a prolonged silence can become the highest form of personal communication, real communion, especially if we both feel we are in God's presence. One might then really say there was such a thing as 'silentiotherapy.'"[9]

—Paul Tournier, *The Adventure of Living*

Inward Silence

"Inward silence requires first to forget one's self, to quiet discordant voices and to master obsessive worry, in the perpetual recommencement of one who is never discouraged because always forgiven. Inward silence renders possible our conversation with Jesus Christ."[10]

—Roger Schutz, *The Rule of Taizé*

The Great Encounter

"Solitude indeed is the place of the great encounter, from which all other encounters derive their meaning. In solitude, we meet God."[11]

—Henri J. Nouwen, *Clowning in Rome*

Landscaping the Schedule

"I cannot tune time to your temperament for you. You should write down what your typical day's schedule tends to be like, and then begin landscaping the schedule to create some places and times of privacy for your regular cultivation of silence, communion with your inner being, and communion with the Eternal in your noisy heart."[12]

—Wayne E. Oates, *Nurturing Silence in a Noisy Heart*

Deliberate Focus

"To be 'silent unto God' does not mean drifting into mere feeling, or sinking into reverse, but deliberately getting into the centre of things and focussing on God."[13]

—Oswald Chambers, *The Place of Help*

The Silence of Love

"At the pole opposed to despair there is the silence of love, the holding of hands of the lovers. The prayer in which the vagueness before words has given place to the pure emptiness after them. The form of communication which opens the simple depth of the soul. It comes in flashes and it can become a lifetime—in prayer just as much as with people. Perhaps it is the only truly universal aspect of language, the only means of communication which was not touched by the curse of Babel. Perhaps it is the one way of being together with others and with the Word in which we have no more foreign accent."[14]

> —Ivan Illich, *Celebration of Awareness*

The Ministry of Silence

"Silence is of many kinds. There is a silence which is the prelude to prayer—the moment of hush and ingathering. There is a silence that tends to quiet the soundless words that fall from the tongue and to calm the noises of the mind and spirit. Every person who is concerned about the discipline of prayer must find the ministry of silence in accordance with his particular needs."[15]

> —Howard Thurman, *Disciplines of the Spirit*

Days of Silence

"The saints were capable of spiritual silence simply because they had not contracted our modern habit of ceaseless talk in their ordinary life. Their days were days of silence, relieved by periods of conversation, while ours are a wilderness of talk with a rare oasis of silence."[16]

> —E. Herman, *Creative Prayer*

A General Emptiness

"Contemplation is essentially a listening in silence, an expectancy. And yet in a certain sense, we must truly begin to hear God when we have ceased to listen. What is the explanation of this paradox? Perhaps only there is a higher kind of listening which is not an attentiveness to some special wave length, a receptivity to a certain kind of message, but a general emptiness that waits to realize the fullness of the message of God within its own apparent void."[17]

> —Thomas Merton, *The Climate of Monastic Prayer*

Silent Expectation

"Before there can be meaningful conversation with God, we must take time to wait on the Lord in silent expectation."[18]

—Donald G. Bloesch, *The Struggle of Prayer*

The Centre Remains Still

"For there is a silent communion that is strangely independent of the tumult of the world outside.

"A famous simile is often used in the East which describes this inner stillness. It is taken from the spinning top in rapid motion. The point is made that, while the top spins round, the centre remains still. So the soul, that is truly poised and centred in God, is able to remain calm amid the whirling rush and din of the outer world."[19]

—C. F. Andrews, *Christ and Prayer*

Your Particular Wilderness

"You are confronted with the necessity of deciding what is your particular wilderness. What *place* or situation in life makes silence a reality? What place gives you freedom from the clamoring noise of other people's opinions, peering eyes, and demanded expectations?"[20]

—Wayne E. Oates, *Nurturing Silence in a Noisy Heart*

A Great Silence

"One September morning (during a stay at 'Jordans,' the Quaker settlement at Buckinghamshire) I got up at a quarter to seven, walked through the kitchen garden, up through the orchard where the owls were still crying, through a gate, and into a meadow. But not only into a meadow, into a great silence. It was in the meadow that I met God."[21]

—Leslie Weatherhead, *A Private House of Prayer*

The Great Quiet of God
"In the castle of my soul
Is a little postern gate
Whereat, when I enter
I am in the presence of God.
In a moment, in the turning of a thought,
I am where God is.
This is a fact.
When I enter into God,
All life has a meaning,
Without asking I know:
My desires are even now fulfilled,
My fever is gone
In the great quiet of God.
My troubles are but pebbles on the road,
My joys are like the everlasting hills.
So it is when I step through the gate of prayer
From time to eternity."[22]

—Walter Rauschenbusch, *First Steps in Prayer*

A Moist Humus
"To preserve the silence within—amid all the noise. To remain open and quiet, a moist humus in the fertile darkness where the rain falls and the grain ripens—no matter how many tramp across the parade ground in whirling dust under an arid sky."[23]

—Dag Hammarskjöld, *Markings*

Some Centering Moment
"We wait in the quietness for some centering moment that will redefine, reshape, and refocus our lives."[24]

—Howard Thurman, *The Centering Moment*

Turning Point

"To ears which have been trained to wait upon God in silence, and in the quietness of meditation and prayer, a very small incident, or a word, may prove to be a turning point in our lives, and a new opening for his love to enter our world, to create and to redeem."[25]

—Olive Wyon, *Prayer*

Be Silent to God

"One translator interprets the command, 'Be still, and know that I am God,' this way: 'Be silent to God and He will mold you.' Be silent to God and He will make and mold you to become the instrument of His purposes."[26]

—E. Stanley Jones, *Abundant Living*

An Overawing Presence

"Prayer . . . should be so deeply inward as often to be lost in a great silence. The act of prayer should appropriately commence and end in such silence, since it is the natural effect of an overawing Presence to still and silence other beings."[27]

—Albert Belden, *The Practice of Prayer*

Silence Is an Act

"We usually think of silence not as an activity but as a state of not talking. But to be silent is an act, and not just a passive state, because to be silent means to attend, to pay attention to another."[28]

—James E. Griffiss, *A Silent Path to God*

The Final Say

"Silence as waiting is the acknowledgement that it is God who has the 'final say' on the outcome of existence."[29]

—Thomas Troeger, *Rage! Reflect. Rejoice!*

First and Last Words

"We are silent at the beginning of the day because God should have the first word, and we are silent before going to sleep because the last word also belongs to God."[30]

—Dietrich Bonhoeffer, *Life Together*

8

Persistence

To Test Desire

"Persistence forces us to test desire and to clarify it in expression. Furthermore, it tests our willingness to focus completely in concentrated awareness upon God to whom the need is offered."[1]

—John B. Magee, *Reality and Prayer*

Getting to Your Door

"Be importunate, Jesus says—not, one assumes, because you have to beat a path to God's door before he'll open it, but because until you beat the path maybe there's no way of getting to *your* door."[2]

—Frederick Buechner, *Wishful Thinking, A Theological ABC*

Our Impassioned Questioning
"The language of prayer is that of our impassioned questioning of God and hence also expresses our tensely anxious affectation that God will one day vindicate the terrible suffering of the world. Protest is fused with unreserved lament, and the tenderness of the language in no way denies its sadness."[3]

—Karl Rahner, *The Courage to Pray*

Laborious Receptivity
"Our cooperation with God is our receptivity; but it is an active, a laborious receptivity, an importunity that drains our strength away. . . ."[4]

—P. T. Forsyth, *The Soul of Prayer*

Wait for an Answer
"Boys on Hallowe'en ring bells and run. So, many of us pray. But any one who has serious business will wait for an answer to his summons and if need be, will ring again. The patient waiting, the reiterated demand are an expression and a test of our earnestness."[5]

—Harry Emerson Fosdick, *The Meaning of Prayer*

Working on God?
"The idea is not our trying to get through to God, but His attempting to get through to us. We may be inclined to think that prayer is our 'working on God,' but it's just the opposite. It works on us, opens us to the pursuing God."[6]

—William Toohey, *Life After Birth*

Until We Are Ready

"God wishes us to strive with him before we submit because he wants to convince us. He desires to see how earnest we really are. He hides the full meaning of his will from us until we are ready to accept it."[7]

—Donald G. Bloesch, *The Struggle of Prayer*

Pleading Is Arguing

"Petition is asking; whereas pleading is arguing. When a petitioner is in dead earnest, he is not content with merely tabling his petition. He does not simply state his bare case, and then leave it to speak for itself. No. Far from that. He at once proceeds to support his case with all the reasons and arguments and appeals that he can command."[8]

—Alexander Whyte, *Lord, Teach Us to Pray*

Whole Life at Stake

"Whoever wrestles with God in prayer puts his whole life at stake. Otherwise it would not be a *genuine* combat, or indeed it would not be a combat *with God.*"[9]

—Jacques Ellul, *Prayer and Modern Man*

Patient with God

"I have always found prayer difficult. So often it seems like a fruitless game of hide and seek in which we seek and God hides. I know God is very patient with me. Without that patience, I should be lost. But frankly I have to be patient with him. With no other friend would I go on seeking with such scant, conscious response. Yet I cannot leave prayer alone for long. My need drives me to him. And I have a feeling that he has his own reasons for hiding himself, and that finally all my seeking will prove infinitely worthwhile."[10]

> —Leslie Weatherhead, *A Private House of Prayer*

Not a Perpetual April

"It is only the sentimentalists who depict prayer as a perpetual April. A good deal of prayer is framed in fall and winter, and much of the real work of prayer is best done in these very seasons."[11]

> —Douglas Steere, *Dimensions of Prayer*

A Cry of Lament

"Again and again prayer is a cry of lament from the depths of the spirit. But this cry is in no sense a vague, rambling moan. It calls out loudly, insistently."[12]

> —Karl Rahner, *The Courage to Pray*

Rugged Human Struggle

"It has been said that the American Black person lives life from one crisis to another. Without doubt, Black prayer language reflects this. Even when circumstances are calm and placid, a Black person's theology will reflect an image of just 'making it through life.' In prayers he or she is forever 'climbing a high mountain' or 'going through a deep valley.' These symbols of rugged human struggle are needed in the mindview of a people whose history has taken them from oppression to the present struggle for liberation."[13]

> —Harold Carter, *The Prayer Tradition of Black People*

Until the Answer Comes

"The most difficult prayer, and the prayer which, therefore, costs us the most striving, is persevering prayer, the prayer which faints not, but continues steadfastly until the answer comes."[14]

—O. Hallesby, *Prayer*

No-Holds-Barred Struggle

"Prayer is wrestling with God. Prayer is taking on, not the heavyweight champion of the world, but the ruler of the universe! It is pitting ourselves against God Almighty. It is stretching every tendon and tensing every muscle of the soul in a no-holds-barred struggle with the Lord."[15]

—Thomas Troeger, *Rage! Reflect. Rejoice!*

The Fuller Scope of God's Will

"We resist what may be only temporarily God's will so that his ultimate will might be brought to light. We wrestle with God in order to discover the fuller scope of his will, and our success in this endeavor is therefore also God's victory."[16]

—Donald G. Bloesch, *The Struggle of Prayer*

So Costly . . . So Enriching

". . . nothing is so costly, so exorbitant, so extortionate, as that which is bought by prayer. While, on the other hand, nothing is so truly and everlastingly enriching as that which is gotten and held by prayer, and by prayer alone."[17]

—Alexander Whyte, *Lord, Teach Us to Pray*

Deepening Faith
    "There is nothing that so much develops faith as to per-
severe in asking through disappointment. If you always get
the blessing you seek at once, or something you recognize
as corresponding to it, your faith will remain at about the level
at which you started. The reason why God calls for perseverance is not, of course, that He wishes to test our faith. He
knows exactly what it is worth. But He may wish to deepen it.
The thing that will most deepen it is to persist with faith
through disappointment."[18]

—William Temple, *Daily Readings from William Temple*

Clinging to God with Strength
    "The curse of so much religion . . . is that men cling to
God with their weakness rather than with their strength."[19]

—P. T. Forsyth, *The Soul of
Prayer*

The Gymnasium of the Soul
    "True prayer will achieve just as much as it cost us. It is
the little further that costs; it is the little further that counts.
. . . The inner chamber into which we retire for daily prayer
is the gymnasium of the soul."[20]

—Samuel Zwemer, *Taking Hold
of God*

Will-Pressure
    "I am like an oarsman rowing against a current. My *will-
pressure must be gentle but constant*, to listen to God, to
pray for others incessantly, to look at people as *souls* and not
as clothes, or bodies, or even minds. The moment the pressure on the oar ceases, I drift, and downward. . . . 'Let go and
let God' does not fit my experience. 'Take hold and keep hold

of God' is what it feels like to me. There is a *will-act,* and I can feel the spiritual muscles growing from rowing."[21]

—Frank Laubach, *Prayer Diary*

Two Wings

"Perseverance and a loving spirit are like the two wings on which prayer soars aloft, and neither of them must be broken."[22]

—C. F. Andrews, *Christ and Prayer*

Its Cost

"Each time you take a human soul with you into your prayer, you accept from God a piece of spiritual work with all of its implications and with all its cost—a cost which may mean for you spiritual exhaustion and darkness, and may even include vicarious suffering, the Cross."[23]

—Evelyn Underhill, *The Evelyn Underhill Reader*

Toughened Fiber

"His 'No' is only in order to a higher 'Yes.' . . . But that 'Yes' may be delayed—delayed in order to put persistence and toughened fiber in us. He often holds us off to deepen our characters, so that we won't be spiritual crybabies if we don't get everything at once."[24]

—E. Stanley Jones, *Abundant Living*

The Petition That Is Heard

"The importunate, obstinate, aggressive petition is heard. A blind man, seated by the wayside, shouted his supplications more and more loudly in spite of those who wanted to silence him. 'Thy faith hath made thee whole,' said Jesus, who was passing that way."[25]

—Alexis Carrel, *Prayer*

An Effort of Will

"Prayer is an effort of will, and the great battle in prayer is the overcoming of mental woolgathering. We put things down to the devil when we should put them down to our inability to concentrate."[26]

—Oswald Chambers, *The Place of Help*

Hard to Reach

"We see that we need to persist, not because God is hard to reach, but because we are. We need to persist in our efforts to listen, to open our hearts and reply to His call."[27]

—William Toohey, *Life After Birth*

A Means of Resistance

"Prayer is a source of opposition, an 'intermission,' a means of resistance to that inexorable continuity which reduces us to apathy and makes us so apolitical (as will be borne out by the technocratic future of our societies), and so makes us incapable of expecting anything."[28]

—Karl Rahner, *The Courage to Pray*

I Cannot Give Up

"Jesus sometimes found prayer difficult. Some of his most agonized prayers were not answered. But he did not give up his praying. I frankly have little to show for all my prayers, but I cannot give up, for 'my soul longeth for God,' and I know that outside God there is nothing at all but death."[29]

—Leslie Weatherhead, *A Private House of Prayer*

Morning Follows

"The dawn will come. Disappointment, sorrow, and despair are born at midnight, but morning follows. . . . This faith adjourns the assemblies of hopelessness and brings new light into the dark chambers of pessimism."[30]

—Martin Luther King, Jr., *Strength to Love*

Eternal Striving

"Prayer is not our meandering search for a missing God; rather, it is our participation in that eternal striving of Father, Son, and Spirit to restore creation's glory which catches us up, even without being aware of it, into the life of the Trinity itself."[31]

—William Hull, *"Prayer: Human and Divine"*

9

Communion

The Center of the Matter
". . . *the thought of prayer as communion with God puts the center of the matter where it ought to be.* The great gift of God in prayer is himself, and whatever else he gives is incidental and secondary."[1]

—Harry Emerson Fosdick, *The Meaning of Prayer*

The Joy of Communion
"Prayer, no doubt, is a great deal more than this inner act of discovery and appreciation of God, but the joy of communion and intercourse with God is the central feature of prayer and it is one of the most impressive facts of life."[2]

—Rufus Jones, *Rufus Jones Speaks to Our Time, An Anthology*

Slow, Very Slow

"In his holy search the holy God did not go on a motorcycle or by supersonic jet. He became *slow,* very slow. The crucifixion of Jesus Christ, the son of God, means that God went so slow that he became nailed down in his search of man. What speed can be slower than the dead stop of being nailed down? If God revealed in such a way his character, man must approach him in the same manner."[3]

—Kosuke Koyama, *50 Meditations*

An Established Residence

"Prayer is not a stratagem for occasional use, a refuge to resort to now and then. It is rather like an established residence for the innermost self. All things have a home: the bird has a nest, the fox has a hole, the bee has a hive. A soul without prayer is a soul without a home."[4]

—Abraham Heschel, *The Wisdom of Heschel*

Necessary to Life

"To be a Christian and to pray are one and the same thing; it is a matter that cannot be left to our caprice. It is a need, a kind of breathing necessary to life."[5]

—Karl Barth, *Prayer According to the Catechisms of the Reformation*

Taking Initiative

"Prayer . . . is not the moment when God and human are in relationship, for that is always. *Prayer is taking initiative to intentionally respond to God's presence.* We can do that with words or with feelings, with intellect or with intuition, alone or with others."[6]

—L. Robert Keck, *The Spirit of Synergy: God's Power and You*

A Life-Giving Relationship

"True communion with the Presence is a healthy and life-giving relationship in which we seek God—not an experience, not an emotion, a mood, or a feeling—in which we renounce any test of ecstasy or illumination as evidence."[7]

—Lance Webb, *The Art of Personal Prayer*

Living to Pray

"But at last it is truer to say that we live the Christian life in order to pray than that we pray in order to live the Christian life."[8]

—P. T. Forsyth, *The Soul of Prayer*

The Fundamental Intent of Life

"When the hunger in a man's heart merges with what seems to be the fundamental intent of life, communion with God the Creator of Life is not only possible but urgent."[9]

—Howard Thurman, *Disciplines of the Spirit*

Indwelling Life

"His life indwells each person . . . and the communion of our separate lives with that frontal love and life is prayer."[10]

—Evelyn Underhill, *The Evelyn Underhill Reader*

A Supreme Moment

"The person who prayed in the Black prayer tradition was always doing three things. First, one was literally talking with God. Such a person was convinced the Spirit was telling him or her what to say. Secondly, one was talking with oneself. A person's own problems, frustrations, yearnings, and expectations came through in the moment of prayer. Thirdly, one was talking with those persons who joined with one in the act of worship. The act of prayer was always a supreme moment when the person's life was literally shared in an act of divine communication."[11]

—Harold Carter, *The Prayer Tradition of Black People*

Fixing Attention Upon God

"Prayer, of course, can never become a habit which needs no attention, for prayer is the fixing of the attention upon God; but it can become perfectly natural for us to do this, so natural that every instant our hearts will turn to God, referring all things to him and seeking his strength and peace."[12]

—Robert Speer, *A Christian's Habits*

Looking at God

"An old peasant was sitting alone in the back pew of an empty church. 'What are you waiting for?' he was asked. 'I am looking at Him,' he answered, 'and He is looking at me.' . . . Every technique of prayer is good which draws man nearer to God."[13]

—Alexis Carrel, *Prayer*

Becoming One

"The person praying becomes truly one with the Person to whom he prays."[14]

—Albert Belden, *The Practice of Prayer*

If . . .

"If you are God's child, there is this expectant line of communication always between you and God. Your experience may be a dreary wilderness, a sea of despair, a dusty, sandy waste with no shade—but over all is a line of communication between you and God." [15]

—Oswald Chambers, *The Place of Help*

Life Itself

"We know that communion with God does not only mean mastery over life, but that it is life itself." [16]

—E. Herman, *Creative Prayer*

In the Presence of God

"To pray . . . does not mean to think about God in contrast to thinking about other things, or to spend time with God instead of spending time with other people. Rather, it means to think and live in the presence of God." [17]

—Henri J. Nouwen, *Clowning in Rome*

In God's Presence

"When we are in God's presence by prayer we are *right*, our will is morally right, we are doing His will." [18]

—P. T. Forsyth, *The Soul of Prayer*

The Religious Act

"This communion with the Supernatural . . . whether active or passive, interceding or adoring—for all these are the partial expressions of one rich and various correspondence—

is the religious act, the religious state *par excellence;* the very substance of a spiritual life."[19]

—Evelyn Underhill, *The Evelyn Underhill Reader*

Quiet Assurance
"With my head in my hands, I bowed over the kitchen table and prayed aloud. . . .

"At that moment I experienced the presence of the Divine as I had never experienced Him before. It seemed as though I could hear the quiet assurance of an inner voice saying: 'Stand up for righteousness, stand up for truth; and God will be at your side forever.' Almost at once my fears began to go. My uncertainty disappeared. I was ready to face anything."[20]

—Martin Luther King, Jr., *Stride Toward Freedom*

Glad Simply to Be with You
"Prayer is being in God's presence and knowing that we don't have to share everything we feel. As a genuine friend and a loving parent, God is glad simply to be with us. We feel the comfort of being understood without being exposed."[21]

—Thomas Troeger, *Rage! Reflect. Rejoice!*

Companionship
"The simplest and most fundamental prayer is an experience of companionship . . . a sense of real companionship with a Friend who is unseen but yet present."[22]

—John Wishart, *The Fact of Prayer*

Approachable by Love

"The simple are conscious of God as naturally as of the warmth of the sun, or the perfume of a flower. But this God, so approachable by him who knows how to love, is hidden from him who knows only how to understand."[23]

—Alexis Carrel, *Prayer*

To Rest in God's Presence

"It is very good to turn aside from the rush and the weariness and the anxieties by which these days beset and lay siege to our moments, to rest in the presence of God."[24]

—Howard Thurman, *The Centering Moment*

Prayer Without an Agenda

"Historically, communion with God simply because God is God has been central to the Christian concept of prayer. We find it in Jesus, Paul, Augustine, Calvin, Barth, and many others. This is prayer without an agenda—concentrated only on fellowship with the living God."[25]

—L. Robert Keck, *The Spirit of Synergy*

Unless and Until

"Service in love is made possible only because of communion with God in prayer. We cannot love our neighbor with the love of God unless and until we are united with God in faith."[26]

—Donald G. Bloesch, *The Struggle of Prayer*

Not a Stranger

"In contemplative prayer, Christ cannot remain a stranger

who lived long ago in a foreign world. Rather, he becomes a living presence with whom we can enter into dialogue here and now."[27]

—Henri J. Nouwen, *Clowning in Rome*

The Culmination

"The culmination of the prayer-life is thus seen to be an active 'walk with God,' a cooperation with Him in practical ways, a communion, not of idea or word or feeling only, but also of action, thus completing the correspondence of the human life with the Divine Life."[28]

—Albert Belden, *The Practice of Prayer*

The Inexpressible Relationship

"When I think of you, Lord, I cannot say whether it is in this place that I find you more, or in that place—whether you are to me Friend or Strength or Matter—whether I am contemplating you or whether I am suffering—whether I rue my faults or find union—whether it is you I love or the whole sum of others. Every affection, every desire, every possession, every light, every depth, every harmony, and every ardour glitters with equal brilliance, at one and the same time, in the inexpressible *Relationship* that is being set up between me and you: Jesus!"[29]

—Pierre Teilhard de Chardin, *Writings in Times of War*

An Inscape

"Prayer is a growing; it is a discovering; it is a communion, a communion most of all with Him in whom all things are. Prayer is an inscape, the totality of the universe experienced in the minutest atom."[30]

—Edward J. Farrell, *Prayer Is a Hunger*

10

Surrender

An Altar and an Oblation

"Prayer at long last is an altar and an oblation. . . . By this surrender prayer finds a 'service which is perfect freedom.' In this loss prayer wins its richest gain."[1]

—George A. Buttrick, *Prayer*

Its Essence

"Grammatically . . . prayer may be in the form of a request ('Be merciful to me, a sinner'). In its essence, however, it is more accurately recognized as an answer, an opening, a surrender."[2]

—William Toohey, *Life After Birth*

A Habit of Surrender

"If an act of devotion opened our soul's floodgates to the

inrush of God's creative energy, shall a life of devotion do less?

"Must it not rather involve the cumulative force of a succession of such acts, and a succession so close as to make of all life a habit of surrender as continuous and inevitable as breathing?"[3]

—E. Herman, *Creative Prayer*

With a Smile
"True holiness consists in doing God's will with a smile."[4]

—Mother Teresa, *A Gift for God*

The Wholly Surrendered
"If we lack a reverent, vital, living expression of this prayer [The Lord's Prayer], our lives will suffer. In it is the secret to great power. But it is not released by vain repetition. Pagans, even though they call themselves by Christ's name, never taste its essence. For this is the prayer of the totally committed, the wholly surrendered, the completely dedicated citizens of the kingdom of God."[5]

—Clarence Jordan, *Sermon on the Mount*

Not Imposing Our Will on God
"Man in prayer does not seek to impose his will upon God; he seeks to impose God's will and mercy upon himself."[6]

—Abraham Heschel, *The Wisdom of Heschel*

Bit by Bit
"This dedication of the will is not easy. It asks from us a persistent, gradual, patient, and ever-deepening surrender to

God's call at every point in our lives. Bit by bit, here a little and there a little, body, mind, and spirit are offered to God."[7]

—Olive Wyon, *Prayer*

A Continual Process

"We lose the 'I-that-is' in order to find the 'I-that-ought-to-be.' This is done by a once-and-for-all surrender, but it is also done as a continual process. The continual process is prayer. Prayer is fundamentally and essentially self-surrender."[8]

—E. Stanley Jones, *Abundant Living*

Adamant in His Commitment

"A young man, adamant in his commitment, who walks the road of possibility to the end without self-pity or demand for sympathy, fulfilling the destiny he has chosen—even sacrificing affection and fellowship when the others are unready to follow him—into a new fellowship."[9]

—Dag Hammarskjöld, *Markings*

Renounce All Claims

"We must not only release our prayer in faith; we must also renounce all claims in an act of humility."[10]

—John B. Magee, *Reality and Prayer*

Take Hands Off

"Don't grit your teeth and clench your fists and say, 'I will! I will!' Relax. Take hands off. Submit yourself to God. Learn to live in the passive voice—a hard saying for Americans— and let life be willed through you."[11]

—Thomas R. Kelly, *A Testament of Devotion*

Simple Turned-Towardness

"We call prayer in the pregnant sense of the term that speech of man to God which, whatever else is asked, ultimately asks for the manifestation of the divine presence, for this presence's becoming dialogically perceivable. The single presupposition of a genuine state of prayer is thus the readiness of the whole man for this presence, simple turned-towardness, unreserved spontaneity."[12]

—Martin Buber, *The Way of Response*

Not at the Right Time

"I have often found that what I sought most I did not get at the right time, not till it was too late, not till I had learned to do without it, till I had renounced it in principle (though not in desire)."[13]

—P. T. Forsyth, *The Soul of Prayer*

One Inexhaustible Theme

"Let us speak to Him as children, confidently and earnestly: 'My Father, I dare to tell Thee that I love Thee.' All prayers of dedication are but expositions and variations of this one inexhaustible theme."[14]

—Karl Rahner, *On Prayer*

Letting Go

"Prayer at its best is the surrender of our little, failing selves to him to be cleansed, renewed, strengthened and led. Like the boatman and the archer, we pray by pulling and pulling until we get our desires in line with his, but the time comes when our prayer is completed by letting go."[15]

—Lance Webb, *The Art of Personal Prayer*

Nearly All Will
"I have a notion that what seem our worst prayers may really be, in God's eyes, our best. Those, I mean, which are least supported by devotional feeling and contend with the greatest disinclination. For these, perhaps, being nearly all will, come from a deeper level than feeling. In feeling there is so much that is really not ours—so much comes from weather and health or from the last book read."[16]

—C. S. Lewis, *Letters to Malcolm: Chiefly on Prayer*

Prayer and Sacrifice
"Our ability to sacrifice ourselves in a mature and generous spirit may well prove to be one of the tests of our interior prayer. Prayer and sacrifice work together. Where there is no sacrifice, there will eventually turn out to be no prayer, and vice versa."[17]

—Thomas Merton, *The Climate of Monastic Prayer*

Not Mass-Produced
"Life with God is the most solid and deep of all reality. So, expect often to be surprised. There are no 'textbook cases' in prayer. No one grows according to a set pattern. We are, after all, not mass-produced but hand-crafted, each one of us. God through Christ treasures and develops our personal uniqueness. The more we belong to him, the more we are 'ourselves.' That, incidentally, is the great difference between the freedom of belonging to God and the bondage of belonging to something else."[18]

—Flora Wuellner, *Prayer and the Living Christ*

The Glory of God
"This is a law of prayer: God can give only to the degree

that we give ourselves to Him. The way of receiving is through giving. But it must be remembered that this giving, this commitment, must be totally for the glory of God and without the slightest thought of receiving."[19]

—John B. Magee, *Reality and Prayer*

No Other Option

"Prayer leads us to see that there is no other option for us than to trust in God. In prayer we find God to be the one absolute security of our life."[20]

—Thomas Troeger, *Rage! Reflect. Rejoice!*

What God Has for Us

"In all true prayer the object is not to impose one's own will upon God, but to discover and accept what God has for us, and it is imperative to keep on trying in spite of failure."[21]

—Georgia Harkness, *Prayer and the Common Life*

What Is Ultimately Right

"Prayer is an invitation to God to intervene in our lives, to let His will prevail in our affairs; it is the opening of a window to Him in our will, an effort to make Him the Lord of our soul. We submit our interests to His concern and seek to be allied with what is ultimately right."[22]

—Abraham Heschel, *The Wisdom of Heschel*

Without Limit to God

"The altar, the place of oblation, where I give myself without limit to God as a reasonable and living sacrifice, and thereby receive from Him new life; the whole drive of my devotional life should be toward that."[23]

—Evelyn Underhill, *The Evelyn Underhill Reader*

To No One but God

"The dissipation of devotion is seen over and over again in the practical issues of our lives. People give their lives to many things they have no business to. No one has any right to give up the right to himself or to herself to anyone but God Almighty. . . ."[24]

—Oswald Chambers, *The Place of Help*

Attuned to Your Will

"God, this attempt to keep my will bent toward your will is integrating me. Here in this Calcutta station, I feel new power such as I have not had for many years. The task to which You have called me is as hard to accomplish as scaling Mount Everest, but you can accomplish it if I can keep my will attuned to Your will."[25]

—Frank Laubach, *Prayer Diary*

A Willing Slave

". . . I will renounce my will, my inclinations, my whims and fancies, and make myself a willing slave to the will of God.[26]

—Mother Teresa, *A Gift for God*

Not Humiliation but Glory

"Kneel or stand before your Creator, as pliable as clay in the potter's hand or as impressionable as marble before a great sculptor or as canvas before a great painter. Ask to be a clear channel for God's spirit to flow through. Surrender to God is not humiliation but glory, through which you become a very necessary means for the completion of God's work. It is a blessed privilege and opportunity to let God's power work through you."[27]

—Kermit Olsen, *First Steps in Prayer*

As One Loves

". . . one prays as one loves, with one's whole being."[28]

—Alexis Carrel, *Prayer*

Putting Back into God's Hands

"God gains a bigger opportunity for His good purposes towards us with every good life that looks up to Him in self-surrender. When we pray passionately and perseveringly and with that consecration of self that real prayer always achieves, we are literally putting back into God's hands the energy and life and being which He surrendered in our creation, and so He gains *increase* of power and *freedom* of action in the human sphere."[29]

—Albert Belden, *The Practice of Prayer*

My Fulfillment

"And therefore, for love's sake, then,
I will do what no power
in heaven or hell or in the earth
could make me do if I did not love.
So, God, as experience must be like this,

I would not snare Thee in a web of words,
I would not try to reduce
all the vast reaches of Thy meaning
to paltry symbols.
I would but open myself to Thee
and let Thy spirit invade me
and fill me until I do not know
what is mine or Thine.
This would be my fulfillment,
O my God!"[30]

—Howard Thurman, *The Centering Moment*

The Tranquil Sea of God's Will

"Let me tell you with the heart of a brother that now more than ever it is a case of closing your eyes and hands, of ridding yourself completely of the baggage of your selfhood and of plunging into the sure and tranquil sea of God's holy will where alone will you find a measure of peace."[31]

—Pope John XXIII, *Wit and Wisdom of Good Pope John*

11

❧❧

Recollection

Recollect and Recall

"Let us recollect for whom, and for what, we prayed in secret this morning—or did not pray. Let us recall what we read, what we heard and with what feelings: with whom we conversed, and about what . . ."[1]

—Alexander Whyte, *Lord, Teach Us to Pray*

Recording the Inward Journey

"There is hardly a master of the religious way who could read and write who did not keep some record of this inward journey. Many of the greatest religious classics were set down originally as journals which these people kept to record their spiritual journeys. They seemed to feel that it showed lack of respect for the source they sought if they came to an encounter with Love and did not make a record of it."[2]

—Morton T. Kelsey, *The Other Side of Silence*

105

What Takes Place Within Us

"A journal's main value often lies not in the entries we make in it, but in what takes place within us as we write. Writing is a proven way of finding out what is going on deep within us. It helps us get in touch with our deeper, unknown selves. It tunes us in to the wordless conversations going on in the sanctuary of our being between God and ourselves."[3]

—Mark Link, *Breakaway*

Write It Down

"If you are willing to commit your prayer to paper, you probably really mean it. In writing it down you do two things: You write it more deeply on your own heart; you commit yourself more fully to a line of action. To write it down is one step in self-committal."[4]

—E. Stanley Jones, *Abundant Living*

Praying by Writing

"Prayer is a hunger, a hunger that is not easily quieted. Today the cry 'teach us to pray' echoes and reverberates from many directions. One of the ways I have learned to pray is by writing. I began by copying favorite passages from reading, then thoughts and ideas of others and finally by jotting down my own insights and reflections from prayer and experiences of each day. This prayer journal at times seems like my own biography of Christ, a kind of Fifth Gospel."[5]

—Edward J. Farrell, *Prayer Is a Hunger*

Written Meditation

"In my experience, the practice of written meditation can be a great help in bridging the gap between our two worlds, the spiritual and the material. . . . Writing something down also makes it more real. If I do not write, my meditation is likely to remain vague and nebulous."[6]

—Paul Tournier, *The Adventure of Living*

The Border Lines of Sleep

"I suggest that we try listening to God on the border lines of sleep. . . . If your own noisy, feverish ideas have subsided enough, there often begins to flow a gentle train of ideas, fresh with the clean flavor of heaven. These lovely ideas rise out of the deep unconscious. Many writers have a pen and paper ready at their bedside to record their inspirations before their treacherous memories lose what comes to them."[7]

—Frank Laubach, *Channels of Spiritual Power*

A Concrete Manifestation

"Over and above its many other values, a prayer journal is a concrete manifestation of a person's all-out, genuine commitment to a program of daily meditation and prayer."[8]

—Mark Link, *Breakaway*

Tools of Spiritual Growth

"Writing is superior to the spoken word in the power to objectify emotion. It is, therefore, no surprise to discover that diaries and spiritual autobiographies have been, for spiritual leaders like Augustine, Fox, or Wesley, tools of spiritual growth. . . . Once we have made the record, we may discover in it, during more tranquil moments, clues of great importance for the self-knowledge that leads to growth."[9]

—John B. Magee, *Reality and Prayer*

This Useful Custom

"How often I have looked over these few pages and felt ashamed to think how badly I have kept the resolve I made . . . to put down on paper some reflections on the state of my conscience. . . .

Now that I have come back from the Easter vacation I have decided, during today's retreat, to resume this useful custom which, with God's help, I hope never to interrupt again." [10]

—Pope John XXIII, *Journal of a Soul*

Improves with Age

"Keeping a journal is one activity on which youth has no corner. It actually improves with age and can continue as long as one is able to hold a pencil or speak into a tape recorder. At thirty, or even fifty, one does not have the depth and wisdom that come in later years. The longer one writes of the depth of self, the more that person finds to write about and the more profound the reflections." [11]

—Morton T. Kelsey, *The Other Side of Silence*

Spiritual Creativity

"Each of us . . . is continually engaged in writing his own personal history. It becomes a real history of the person, however, when it is motivated by spiritual creativity. At no point in experience does man come face to face with this aspect of his being more completely than when he accepts the disciplines of prayer and seeks the fruits of prayerful living. Prayer is the process that develops the sensitivity of the inner kingdom, relates it to its ultimate cosmic meaning, and fulfills that meaning in all of life's relationship. To write one's spiritual biography without prayer is beyond imagination." [12]

—Edgar N. Jackson, *Understanding Prayer*

From the Heart

"Meditation was above all *meditatio scripturarum*. But we must not imagine the early monks applying themselves to a very intellectual and analytical 'meditation' of the Bible. Meditation for them consisted in making the words of the Bible their own by memorizing them and repeating them, with deep and simple concentration 'from the heart.'"[13]

> —Thomas Merton, *The Climate of Monastic Prayer*

A Worthy Investment

"It is much to be regretted that the practice of learning by heart (prayers, Bible passages, poetry, even points from the catechism) does not commend itself to our generation. All who adopt it know it to be a spiritual investment that proves its worth continually."[14]

> —J. Neville Ward, *The Use of Praying*

Memorized Vocabulary

"Spontaneous prayer can come only from lips accustomed to speaking words about God and his people. Inescapably, to do so requires a memorized body of oral traditional materials to provide vocabulary. Rich prayer is kindled with biblical knowledge. Knowing the rich promises of God in Scripture always provides a relevant stand on which one can plead before God."[15]

> —Harold Carter, *The Prayer Tradition of Black People*

Saturate Our Memories

"In every great classic of devotion the author points us back to the Bible and to Christ. The classics must not be given only a single reading. Rather we need to saturate our minds and memories with an author, reading and re-reading over a period of years. Each time we return to a work we discover much to which we were blind before."[16]

—Charles Whiston, *Pray, A Study of Distinctively Christian Praying*

The Fountain of Prayer

"One of the most effective ways in which the spiritual interests of a parishioner may be widened in the practice of prayer is through a daily reading of the Bible. . . . The sublime spiritual truths of the Bible and the effective manner in which it searches out the deep things of the human heart causes the fountain of prayer to well up within the reader."[17]

—John S. Bonnell, *Psychology for Pastor and People*

Reading and Inwardly Digesting

"Men and women who have known and loved God in their day have left accounts of their experiences to help us to know and love him in our day. One of the great aids to progress in prayer, therefore, is the reading and inwardly digesting of the experiences of those who have walked with God. Although the forms of expression may differ from generation to generation, the knowledge and the love are the same, offered to God by men of every age."[18]

—John B. Coburn, *Prayer and Personal Religion*

A Powerful Aid

"Mental prayer or meditation is not a substitute for true prayer, nor is it to be regarded as a higher form of prayer. Yet rightly understood it can be a powerful aid in prayer. It can be a preparation for prayer as well as a supplement to it."[19]

—Donald G. Bloesch, *The Struggle of Prayer*

Hear God and Do It

"Open before me are the words of Luke 8:18 and 21: 'Take heed therefore how ye hear' and 'My mother and my brethren are these which hear the word of God and do it.' 'Hear God and do it' is the center of this year's effort to hear and do, *every* instant of my waking day."[20]

—Frank Laubach, *Prayer Diary*

A Point of Embarkation

"He who would be a man of prayer must regularly return to the Bible as a point of embarkation for his meditation because, for one who stands in our tradition, the Bible is the place where the primary lode is to be mined."[21]

—John Yungblut, *Rediscovering Prayer*

The Record of God's Meeting

"So it is with Bible reading. . . . We need to read in a prayerful mood. . . . Openings and insights will come when and where Christ chooses to give them . . . it is helpful to underline the words or make a marginal notation to remind us, in future rereadings, of the words that have brought about these meetings with Christ. . . . Such entries will over the years become one's very own personal, living concordance of Scripture passages, very different from the objective concordances of scholars. Here is the record of God's meeting and speaking to one directly through the Bible's words."[22]

—Charles Whiston, *Pray, A Study of Distinctively Christian Praying*

Open Your Eyes

". . . never open your New Testament till you have offered this prayer to God the Holy Ghost: 'Open Thou mine eyes!'

And then, as you read, stop and ponder; stop and open your eyes: stop and imagine; stop till you actually *see* Jesus Christ in the same room with you. 'Lo! I am with you alway!'"[23]

—Alexander Whyte, *Lord, Teach Us to Pray*

Play upon the Material
"Meditation . . . is the intentional, yet not coerced, effort to read or think about, to read *and* think about, some significant incident in God's way with men as reported in Scripture or in some other piece of writing. . . . One lets his mind play upon the material until it speaks significantly and helpfully."[24]

—Norman Pittenger, *Praying Today*

Scripture Before Prayer
"Perhaps the most characteristic quality of Jewish prayer is its emphasis on Torah-learning. In the daily morning services, the benediction for Torah follows immediately after the benedictions expressing gratitude for the varied gifts of life. And the faithful Jew is expected to read selected passages from Scripture and the writings of the sages before he begins his prayers."[25]

—Jacob Agus, *Great Jewish Ideas*

Perspective and Depth
"In addition to a bit of reflection or contemplation every day, we must also set aside longer periods of time at intervals in our life to get more perspective and more depth. In the absence of experiences like an annual retreat or several days of recollection a year, I fear that we are going to run out of spiritual energy."[26]

—Andrew M. Greeley, *Letters to Nancy*

The Watering of Our Roots

"Surrounded by all of the memories and the dreams and the hopes and the desires of so great a host of witnesses, we still ourselves in the presence of God, gathering together all of the things that are needful for our peace. The mood of thanksgiving overwhelms us when we remember how good and great is our fortune, even as we are mindful of the ways that are hard and difficult for so many whose names are known to us and whose pictures are vividly in our minds. It is so great a privilege to experience the watering of one's roots at a time of such dryness in the world."[27]

—Howard Thurman, *The Centering Moment*

Withdrawal and Rumination

"Self-awareness in prayer is usually thought of as an attitude of recollectedness, but what it really means is welcoming the Spirit in secrecy and silence. . . . The life of prayer needs this experience of withdrawal and rumination."[28]

—Patrick Jacquemont, *"Is Action Prayer?"*

Journal Keeping Is Prayer

"The journal calls for honesty, for a search into meaning. It is a discipline in a day when discipline is rare. 'But it is a narrow gate, and a hard road that leads to life, and only a few find it' Mt. 7, 14. Time set aside to move from the outer to the inner, to discover new depths, to see new connections, to perceive fresh insight—surely this work is prayer."[29]

—Edward J. Farrell, *Prayer Is a Hunger*

12

Action

Ready to Act in Love
". . . the purpose of prayer is to bring God's human child, now become adult in responsibility and thus asked to act in mature ways, into cooperative awareness of God, opened to his love and ready to act in love toward others."[1]

—Norman Pittenger, *Praying Today*

The Integrated Life
"Life and prayer become integrated when prayer issues in service, and when service drives us to prayer."[2]

—Olive Wyon, *Prayer*

The Road of Holiness
"In our era, the road to holiness necessarily passes through the world of action."[3]

—Dag Hammarskjöld, *Markings*

The Light of God

"Prayer does not blind us to the world, but it transforms our vision of the world, and makes us see it, all men, all the history of mankind, in the light of God."[4]

—Thomas Merton, *The Climate of Monastic Prayer*

No Spiritual Transition

"There ought to be no sense of spiritual transition as we pass from any occupation which is our proper occupation at the time, to the thought of God. We should feel, whether it be in performing the duty He has given us or in remembering Him who gave us the duty, that we are always seeking to deepen our union with Him. But the moments when we concentrate upon this purpose particularly are our times of prayer."[5]

—William Temple, *Daily Readings from William Temple*

Noble Action

"Solitude is no longer the road for the man who strives, and true prayer, prayer which steers a course straight for the Lord's house and enters, is noble action. This, today, is how the true warrior prays."[6]

—Nikos Kazantzakis, *Report to Greco*

Prayer Before Battle

"Prayer in the past, like the hiss of escaping steam, has often dissipated moral energy. But prayer before battle is another thing. That has been the greatest breeder of revolutionary heroism in history. All our bravest desires stiffen into fighting temper when they are affirmed before God."[7]

—Walter Rauschenbusch, *Prayers of the Social Awakening*

Praying and Loving

"Many people are troubled because they do not know how to witness. They cannot use the language that the minister uses. Never mind; *the greatest witness is kindness and helpfulness*. If you pray for others enough and love them enough, they will not need words. In the heart of every man and woman there is some need, a longing to be understood, or some other need."[8]

—Frank Laubach, *Channels of Spiritual Power*

Apart from Prayer

"Apart from prayer, action is necessarily violence and falsehood. . . . Prayer is the only possible substitute for violence in human relations."[9]

—Jacques Ellul, *Prayer and Modern Man*

Thinking, Working and Praying

". . . there are three chief ways in which men cooperate with God: thinking, working and praying. Now, no one of these three can ever take the place of the other."[10]

—Harry Emerson Fosdick, *The Meaning of Prayer*

Only Soliloquy

"Prayer that does not bear fruit in self-giving service is not Christian prayer but only soliloquy."[11]

—Donald G. Bloesch, *The Struggle of Prayer*

Working Out
"Prayer is the working out of what God works in."[12]

—E. Stanley Jones, *Abundant Living*

Apostolic Activity
"It is not possible to engage in the direct apostolate without being a soul of prayer. We must be aware of oneness with Christ as he was aware of oneness with the Father. Our activity is truly apostolic only in so far as we permit him to work in us and through us, with his power, with his desire, with his love."[13]

—Mother Teresa, *A Gift for God*

The Needs of the Oppressed
"To believe that we can approach God in any other way, especially prayer, without having heard (responded to) the needs of the oppressed is to believe God will hear our needs when we have been deaf to those of his people."[14]

—Michael H. Crosby, *Thy Will Be Done, Praying the Our Father as Subversive Activity*

Out of Touch with Reality
"What we find is this: With an old notion of prayer, a lot of people were inclined to leave their problems with God, unload their wants and needs upon Him, and then go on living as if nothing had happened.

"That notion of prayer can weaken or detract from our service in the world. It can reduce our will to solve our own problems, by tempting us to leave in God's hand what has actually been placed in our own. For example, we may be so out of touch with reality as to say to God, 'Please feed the hungry people,' without realizing that, if we would only listen,

God is saying to us, 'Don't expect Me to take on your task. *You* feed the hungry people.'"[15]

—William Toohey, *Life After Birth*

Participation

"Christianity leaves the famous distinction between action and contemplation far behind: it is participation; its prayer is love in action and its action is inspired by love."[16]

—Louis Evely, *Our Prayer*

Times of Testing

"Every day brings to the Christian many hours in which he will be alone in an unchristian environment. These are the times of *testing*. This is the test of true meditation and true Christian community. . . . Has it transported him for a moment into a spiritual ecstasy that vanishes when everyday life returns, or has it lodged the Word of God so securely and deeply in his heart that it holds and fortifies him, impelling him to active love, to obedience, to good works? Only the day can decide.[17]

—Dietrich Bonhoeffer, *Life Together*

Concentrate on Loving

"I have known the satisfaction of unrestrained action, and the joy of the contemplative life in the dazzling peace of the desert. . . . Don't worry about what you ought to do. Worry about loving. Don't interrogate heaven repeatedly and uselessly saying, 'What course of action should I pursue?' Concentrate on loving instead.

"And by loving you will find out what is for you."[18]

—Carlo Carretto, *Letters from the Desert*

Bundles of Concern

"But in our love of people are we to be excitedly hurried, sweeping all men and tasks into our loving concern? No, that is God's function. But He, working within us, portions out His vast concern into bundles, and lays on each of us our portion. These become our tasks. Life from the Center is a heaven-directed life."[19]

—Thomas R. Kelly, *A Testament of Devotion*

Ashen Fruits of Disgust

"Meditation has no point and no reality unless it is firmly rooted in *life*. Without such roots, it can produce nothing but the ashen fruits of disgust, *acedia*, and even morbid and degenerate introversion, masochism, dolorism, negation. Nietzche pitilessly exposed the hopeless mess which results from this caricature of Christianity."[20]

—Thomas Merton, *The Climate of Monastic Prayer*

God's Perspective

"Prayer in the Christian sense does not remove us from the world but enables us to see the world in the perspective of God's plan and purpose for it."[21]

—Donald G. Bloesch, *The Struggle of Prayer*

A Causal Relationship

"If a man, after praying, conducts himself differently from before, there is a causal relationship here which science ought to study and recognize."[22]

—Paul Tournier, *The Person Reborn*

Making a Prophet
"Prayer should make a prophet of each one of us."[23]

—Louis Evely, *Our Prayer*

Prayer as an Excuse
". . . I take prayer too seriously to use it as an excuse for avoiding work and responsibility."[24]

—Martin Luther King, Jr., *The Trumpet of Conscience*

Crib and Cross
". . . at Christmas, God comes to us in the depths. I do not need first to have religious feelings, out of which I then produce some internal and external results, before he comes to me. He comes in the stable, to the disconsolate, the sick, and the despairing; he trudges in the long lines of refugees; and if everyone and everything should desert me in my final hour, I can say, 'If I should have to depart, depart not from me.' Then he comes even to the dark valley of death. Crib and cross are of the same wood."[25]

—Helmut Thielicke, *Being a Christian When the Chips Are Down*

Along with God
"Prayer is not an excuse for being lazy and for pushing all the work off on to God; prayer is a way to finding the strength and ability to do things along with God that we could never have done by ourselves."[26]

—William Barclay, *Prayers for Young People*

God's Agents

". . . it is all too easy for us to pray, let us say, for peace or for the unfortunate, and to leave it at that. But true prayer can never encourage sloth. It must rather excite the desire to be God's agents for the fulfilling of the prayer. Prayer never delivers us from action directed towards the end of the prayer. Indeed, prayer would be little more than hypocrisy if it did not issue in such action, and the prayer of asking is only justifiable if we are honestly striving ourselves to realize its objective."[27]

—John Macquarrie, *The Humility of God*

What Is the Value?

"What is the value of praying for the poor if all the rest of our time and interest is given only to becoming rich?"[28]

—P. T. Forsyth, *The Soul of Prayer*

"My Legs Were Praying"

"The support of justice and humanness in our world is certainly a form of prayer and essential to communion with God. Rabbi Abraham Heschel has said, 'When I marched with Martin Luther King in Selma, I felt my legs were praying.'"[29]

—L. Robert Keck, *The Spirit of Synergy*

Praying Is Living

"Prayer leads you to see new paths, to hear new melodies in the air. Prayer is the breath of your life which gives you freedom to go and stay where you wish and to find the many signs which point out the way to a new land. Praying is not simply some necessary compartment in the daily schedule of a Christian or a source of support in time of need, nor is it restricted to Sunday morning or as a frame to surround meal times. Prayer is living."[30]

—Henri J. M. Nouwen, *With Open Hands*

Continuity . . . Prayer . . . Life
"Pray so that there is a real continuity between your prayer and your whole actual life."[31]

—P. T. Forsyth, *The Soul of Prayer*

Notes

Introduction

1. P. T. Forsyth, *The Soul of Prayer* (London: Independent Press LTD, 1954), p. 16

Chapter 1 Preparation

1. Madeleine L'Engle, "The Gift of Prayer," *A.D.*, April, 1980, p. 28.

2. Karl Barth, *Prayer According to the Catechisms of the Reformation,* trans. Sara F. Terrien (Philadelphia: The Westminster Press, 1952), p. 20. Copyright, MCMLII, by W.L. Jenkins. Used by permission of The Westminster Press.

3. Douglas Steere, *Dimensions of Prayer* (New York: Harper & Row, Publishers, Inc., 1962), pp. 14-15.

4. Dietrich Bonhoeffer, *The Cost of Discipleship* (New York: Macmillan, Inc., 1963), p. 181.

5. Lionel Blue, *To Heaven with Scribes and Pharisees: The Jewish Path to God* (New York: Oxford University Press, 1975), pp. 62-63. Copyright © 1975 by Lionel Blue. Reprinted by permission of Dartman, Longman & Todd Ltd, and Oxford University Press.

6. James E. Griffiss, *A Silent Path to God* (Philadelphia: Fortress Press, 1980), p. 70.

7. Elton Trueblood, *The Lord's Prayers* (New York: Harper & Row, Publishers, Inc., 1965), p. 50. Copyright © 1965 by Elton Trueblood. Reprinted by permission of Harper & Row, Publishers, Inc.

8. Charles Henry Brent, *Things That Matter* (New York: Harper & Row, Publishers, Inc., 1949), p. 44. Reprinted by permission of Harper & Row, Publishers, Inc.

9. Jacques Ellul, *Prayer and Modern Man* (New York: The Seabury Press, Inc., 1970), p. 146. Used by permission of The Seabury Press, Inc.

10. Thomas R. Kelly, *A Testament of Devotion* (New York: Harper & Row, Publishers, Inc., 1941), p. 98. Reprinted by permission of Harper & Row, Publishers, Inc.

11. Michael H. Crosby, *Thy Will Be Done: Praying the Our Father as Subversive Activity* (Maryknoll, N. Y.: Orbis Books, 1977), p. 40.

12. P. T. Forsyth, *The Soul of Prayer*, p. 78.

13. H. A. Williams, *The Simplicity of Prayer* (Philadelphia: Fortress Press, 1977), p. 41.

14. Clarence Jordan, *Sermon on the Mount* (Valley Forge: Judson Press, 1970), pp. 83-84. Used by permission of Judson Press.

15. Elizabeth O'Connor, *Journey Inward, Journey Outward* (New York: Harper & Row, Publishers, Inc., 1968), p. 22. Copyright © 1968 by Elizabeth O'Connor. Reprinted by permission of Harper & Row, Publishers, Inc.

16. Arthur Gossip, *In the Secret Place of the Most High* (New York: Charles Scribner's Sons, 1947), p. 90.

17. Frank Laubach, *Channels of Spiritual Power* (Old Tappan, N. J.: Fleming H. Revell Co., 1954), p. 95.

18. Anthony Bloom, *Beginning to Pray* (New York: Paulist Press, 1970), p. 49.

19. Roger Schutz, *The Rule of Taizé* (France: The Communauté de Taizé, 1961), p. 20.

20. Mother Teresa, *A Gift for God* (New York: Harper & Row, Publishers, Inc., 1975), p. 84. Copyright © 1975 by Mother Teresa, Missionaries of Charity. Reprinted by permission of Harper & Row, Publishers, Inc.

21. Morton T. Kelsey, *The Other Side of Silence* (New York: Paulist Press, 1976), p. 92.

22. Gordon Cosby, *Handbook for Mission Groups* (Waco, Tex.: Word Inc., 1975), p. 78.

23. J. Neville Ward, *The Use of Praying* (London: The Epworth Press, 1967), p. 132.

24. Charlie Shedd, *Time for All Things* (Nashville: Abingdon Press, 1962), p. 34. Copyright © 1962 by Abingdon Press. Used by permission.

25. William Axling, *Kagawa* (New York: Harper & Row, Publishers, Inc., 1932), p. 164. Copyright © 1932, 1946 by Harper & Row, Publishers, Inc. Reprinted by permission of Harper & Row, Publishers, Inc.

26. Orien Johnson, *Becoming Transformed* (Valley Forge: Judson Press, 1973), p. 80.

27. James Angell, *When God Made You, He Knew What He Was Doing* (Old Tappan, N. J.: Fleming H. Revell Co., 1972), p. 166.

28. Reuel Howe, *Herein Is Love* (Valley Forge: Judson Press, 1961), p. 86.

29. Karol Wojtyla (Pope John Paul II), *Sign of Contradiction* (New York: The Crossroad Publishing Co., 1979), p. 149.

30. Harry Emerson Fosdick, *The Meaning of Prayer* (New York: Association Press, 1925), pp. 17-18.

31. Nikos Kazantzakis, *Report to Greco* (New York: Simon & Schuster, Inc., 1965), p. 511.

Chapter 2 Adoration

1. Olive Wyon, *Prayer* (Philadelphia: Fortress Press, 1960), p. 61.

2. John Yungblut, *Rediscovering Prayer* (New York: The Seabury Press, Inc., 1972), p. 158.

3. Frederick Buechner, *The Hungering Dark* (New York: The Seabury Press, Inc., 1969), p. 13. Used by permission of the publisher.

4. Donald G. Bloesch, *The Struggle of Prayer* (San Francisco: Harper & Row, Publishers, Inc., 1980), pp. 55-56. Copyright © 1980 by Donald G. Bloesch. Reprinted by permission of Harper & Row, Publishers, Inc.

5. *The Wisdom of Heschel.* Selected by Ruth Marcus Goodhill (New York: Farrar, Straus & Giroux, Inc., 1975), p. 209. Reprinted by permission of Farrar, Straus and Giroux, Inc. Copyright © 1970, 1972, 1975 by Sylvia Heschel, Executrix of the Estate of Abraham Joshua Heschel.

6. Dag Hammarskjöld, *Markings.* Trans. Leif Sjoberg and W. H. Auden (New York: Alfred A. Knopf, Inc., 1964), p. 15. Copyright © 1964 by Alfred A. Knopf, Inc., and Faber & Faber, Ltd. Reprinted by permission of Alfred A. Knopf, Inc.

7. Lance Webb, *The Art of Personal Prayer* (Nashville: Abingdon Press, 1962), p. 18.

8. David Read, *Holy Common Sense* (Nashville: Abingdon Press, 1966), p. 29.

9. Howard Thurman, *Disciplines of the Spirit* (New York: Harper & Row, Publishers, Inc., 1963), pp. 101-102.

10. Thomas Troeger, *Rage! Reflect. Rejoice! Praying with the Psalmists* (Philadelphia: The Westminster Press, 1977), p. 85. Copyright © 1977 The Westminster Press. Used by permission.

11. Clovis G. Chappell, *Sermons on the Lord's Prayer* (Nashville: Abingdon Press, 1934), p. 51.

12. William E. Hulme, *Let the Spirit In* (Nashville: Abingdon Press, 1979), pp. 50-51.

13. John B. Coburn, *Prayer and Personal Religion* (Philadelphia: The Westminster Press, 1957), p. 32.

14. Norman Pittenger, *Praying Today* (Grand Rapids, Mich.: Wm. B. Eerdmans Publishing Co., 1974), p. 56. Used by permission.

15. Martin Luther King, Jr., *Strength to Love* (New York: Harper & Row, Publishers, Inc., 1963), p. 141.

16. Walter Rauschenbusch, *Prayers of the Social Awakening* (Boston: The Pilgrim Press, 1909), p. 47.

17. Edward J. Farrell, *Prayer Is a Hunger* (Denville, N. J.: Dimension Books, Inc., 1972), p. 70.

18. Henri J. Nouwen, *Clowning in Rome* (Garden City, N. Y.: Image Books, a division of Doubleday & Company, Inc., 1979), p. 73. Copyright © 1979 by Henri J. M. Nouwen. Reprinted by permission of Doubleday & Company, Inc.

19. Helmut Thielicke, *Our Heavenly Father: Sermons on the Lord's Prayer,* trans. John W. Doberstein (New York: Harper & Row, Publishers, Inc., 1960), p. 52. Copyright © 1960 by John W. Doberstein. Reprinted by permission of Harper & Row, Publishers, Inc.

20. Mother Teresa, *A Gift for God,* p. 31.

21. Hugh C. Warner, comp., *Daily Readings from William Temple* (New York: Macmillan, Inc., 1950), p. 7. Reprinted by permission of Hodder and Stoughton Limited.

22. George A. Buttrick, *Prayer* (Nashville: Abingdon Press, 1942), p. 217. Copyright renewal © 1970 by George Buttrick. Used by permission of the publisher, Abingdon Press.

23. Excerpted from C. S. Lewis, *Letters to Malcolm: Chiefly on Prayer* (New York: Harcourt Brace Jovanovich, Inc., 1963), pp. 89-90. Copyright © 1963, 1964 by the Estate of C. S. and/or C. S. Lewis. Reprinted by permission of Harcourt, Brace Jovanovich, Inc.

24. Thomas S. Kepler, comp., *The Evelyn Underhill Reader* (Nashville: Abingdon Press, 1962), p. 115. Copyright © 1962 by Abingdon Press. Used by permission.

25. Frank Cumbers, ed., *Daily Readings from the Works of Leslie Weatherhead* (Nashville: Abingdon Press, 1968), p. 332.

26. John Killinger, *Bread for the Wilderness, Wine for the Journey* (Waco, Tex.: Word, Inc., 1976), p. 32. Used by permission of Word Books, Publisher, Waco, Texas 76796.

27. John Casteel, *The Promise of Prayer* (New York: Association Press, 1957), p. 40.

28. Alexander Solzhenitsyn, *A Pictorial Autobiography* (New York: Farrar, Straus & Giroux, 1974), p. 88. © Editions du Seuil, 1974. English translation © 1974 by Farrar, Straus and Giroux, Inc.

Chapter 3 Confession

1. Frederick Buechner, *Wishful Thinking, A Theological ABC* (New York: Harper & Row, Publishers, Inc., 1973), p. 15. Copyright © 1973 by Frederick Buechner. Reprinted by permission of Harper & Row, Publishers, Inc.

2. John B. Coburn, *Prayer and Personal Religion,* p. 40.

3. Lance Webb, *The Art of Personal Prayer,* p. 37.

4. Howard Thurman, *Disciplines of the Spirit,* p. 103.

5. Thomas R. Kelly, *A Testament of Devotion,* p. 50. Reprinted by permission of Harper & Row, Publishers, Inc.

6. J. Neville Ward, *The Use of Praying,* p. 43.

7. Roger Hazelton, *The Root and Flower of Prayer* (New York: Macmillan, Inc., 1943), pp. 81-82.

8. J. Neville Ward, *The Use of Praying,* p. 43.

9. John S. Bonnell, *Psychology for Pastor and People* (New York: Harper & Row, Publishers, Inc., 1948), p. 195. Reprinted by permission of Harper & Row, Publishers, Inc.

10. Karl Barth, *Prayer According to the Catechisms of the Reformation,* p. 71.

11. George A. Buttrick, *Prayer,* pp. 209-210.

12. C. S. Lewis, *Letters to Malcolm: Chiefly on Prayer,* p. 107.

13. Thomas Merton, *The Climate of Monastic Prayer* (Kalamazoo, Mich.: Cistercian Publications, 1969), p. 96.

14. C. F. Andrews, *Christ and Prayer* (New York: Harper & Row, Publishers, Inc., 1937), p. 82.

15. Flora Wuellner, *Prayer and the Living Christ* (Nashville: Abingdon Press, 1969), p. 74. Copyright © 1969 by Abingdon Press. Used by permission.

16. John Casteel, *The Promise of Prayer,* p. 45.

17. John B. Magee, *Reality and Prayer* (Nashville: Abingdon Press, 1957), p. 56. Copyright © 1957 by John Magee. Used by permission of the publisher, Abingdon Press.

18. Arthur Gossip, *In the Secret Place of the Most High,* p. 110.

19. E. Herman, *Creative Prayer* (New York: Harper & Row, Publishers, Inc., n. d.), p. 209. Reprinted by permission of Harper & Row, Publishers, Inc.

20. Harry Emerson Fosdick, *The Meaning of Prayer*, pp. 80-81.

21. Charles Whiston, *Pray, A Study of Distinctively Christian Praying* (Grand Rapids, Mich.: Wm. B. Eerdmans Publishing Co., 1972), p. 94. Used by permission.

22. Thomas Troeger, *Rage! Reflect. Rejoice!*, p. 31.

23. George S. Stewart, *The Lower Levels of Prayer* (Nashville: Abingdon Press, 1939), p. 106.

24. George A. Buttrick, *Prayer*, p. 219.

25. O. Hallesby, *Prayer* (Minneapolis: Augsburg Publishing House, 1931), p. 25. Reprinted by permission of Augsburg Publishing House.

26. Georgia Harkness, *Prayer and the Common Life* (Nashville: Abingdon Press, 1948), p. 57. Copyright renewal © 1975 by Verna Miller. Used by permission of the publisher, Abingdon Press.

27. Dag Hammarskjöld, *Markings*, p. 124.

28. C. F. Andrews, *Christ and Prayer*, pp. 147-148.

29. Dietrich Bonhoeffer, *Life Together*, trans. John W. Doberstein (New York: Harper & Row, Publishers, Inc., 1954), p. 74. Reprinted by permission of the publisher.

30. John B. Magee, *Reality and Prayer*, p. 73.

31. Thomas Troeger, *Rage! Reflect. Rejoice!*, p. 32.

Chapter 4 Thanksgiving

1. Arthur Gossip, *In the Secret Place of the Most High*, p. 75.

2. C. F. Andrews, *Christ and Prayer*, p. 147.

3. Kermit Olsen, *First Steps in Prayer* (Old Tappan, N. J.: Fleming H. Revell Co., 1942), p. 99.

4. Ladislaus Boros, *Christian Prayer* (New York: A Crossroad Book, The Seabury Press, Inc., 1976), p. 22.

5. Anthony Bloom, *Beginning to Pray*, p. 46.

6. Karl Barth, *Prayer According to the Cathechisms of the Reformation*, p. 24.

7. George A. Buttrick, *Prayer*, p. 215.

8. Michel Quoist, *Prayers*, trans. Agnes M. Forsyth and Anne Marie de Commaille (New York: Sheed and Ward, imprint of Andrews & McMeel, Inc., Fairway, Kans., 1963), p. 61.

9. William Toohey, *Life After Birth, Spirituality for College Students* (New York: The Seabury Press, Inc., 1980), p. 96. Used by permission of The Seabury Press, Inc.

10. J. Neville Ward, *The Use of Praying*, p. 21.

11. Orien Johnson, *Becoming Transformed*, p. 65.

12. Roger Hazelton, *The Root and Flower of Prayer*, p. 20.

13. O. Hallesby, *Prayer*, p. 139.

14. Harold Carter, *The Prayer Tradition of Black People* (Valley Forge: Judson Press, 1976), p. 62. Used by permissioin of Judson Press.

15. Arthur Gossip, *In the Secret Place of the Most High*, p. 90.

16. W. Graham Scroggie, *Method in Prayer* (New York: George H. Doran Company, 1916), p. 141.

17. Georgia Harkness, *Prayer and the Common Life*, p. 52.

18. Albert Wieand, *The Gospel of Prayer* (Grand Rapids, Mich.: Wm. B. Eerdmans Publishing Co., 1953), p. 188. Used by permission.

19. Ladislaus Boros, "Prerequisites for Christian Prayer," *The Prayer Life*, ed. Christian Duquoc and Claude Geffré (New York: Herder and Herder, 1972), p. 60.

20. Norman Pittenger, *Praying Today, Practical Thoughts on Prayer* (Grand Rapids, Mich.: Wm. B. Eerdmans Publishing Co., 1974), p. 53. Used by permission.

21. Martin Buber, *The Way of Response: Martin Buber*, ed. Nahum N. Glatzer (New York: Schocken Books, 1966), p. 209. Reprinted by permission of Schocken Books, Inc.

22. Pope John XXIII, *Journal of a Soul*, trans. Dorothy White (New York: McGraw-Hill Book Co., 1964), p. 87.

23. William Barclay, *Prayers for Young People* (New York: Harper & Row, Publishers, Inc., 1963), p. 13. Copyright © 1963 by William Barclay. Reprinted by permission of Harper & Row, Publishers, Inc.

24. Louis Cassels, *Haircuts and Holiness* (Nashville: Abingdon Press, 1972), pp. 124-125.

25. Howard Thurman, *The Centering Moment* (New York: Harper & Row, Publishers, Inc., 1969), p. 22. Copyright © 1969 by Howard Thurman. Reprinted by permission of Harper & Row, Publishers, Inc.

26. John Casteel, *The Promise of Prayer*, p. 64.

27. James E. Griffiss, *A Silent Path to God*, p. 80.

28. Arthur Gossip, *In the Secret Place of the Most High*, p. 76.

29. Hugh Warner, comp., *Daily Readings from William Temple*, p. 117.

30. George S. Stewart, *The Lower Levels of Prayer*, p. 71.

Chapter 5 Petition

1. James E. Griffiss, *A Silent Path to God*, p. 51.

2. Karl Rahner and Johann Baptist Metz, *The Courage to Pray* (New York: The Crossroad Publishing Co., 1981), p. 3.

3. Flora Wuellner, *Prayer and the Living Christ*, p. 96.

4. George A. Buttrick, *Prayer*, p. 220.

5. John Macquarrie, *The Humility of God* (Philadelphia: The Westminster Press), p. 43. © John Macquarrie 1978. Used by permission of The Westminster Press, Philadelphia, PA.

6. William Barclay, *A Spiritual Autobiography* (Grand Rapids, Mich.: Wm. B. Eerdmans Publishing Co., 1975), p. 47. Used by permission.

7. Frank Laubach, *Channels of Spiritual Power*, p. 38.

8. Douglas Steere, *Dimensions of Prayer*, p. 67.

9. Robert Speer, *A Christian's Habits* (Philadelphia: The Westminster Press, 1911), p. 111.

10. Alexis Carrel, *Prayer* (New York: Morehouse-Gorham Co., 1948), pp. 37-38.

11. Henry Sloane Coffin, *Joy in Believing, Selections of Henry Sloane Coffin*, ed. Walter Russell Bowie (New York: Charles Scribner's Sons, 1956), pp. 32-33. Copyright © by Dorothy Prentice Coffin. Reprinted with the permission of Charles Scribner's Sons.

12. P. T. Forsyth, *The Soul of Prayer*, p. 65.

13. C. S. Lewis, *Letters to Malcolm: Chiefly on Prayer*, p. 59.

14. John B. Magee, *Reality and Prayer*, p. 125.

15. Louis Cassels, *Haircuts and Holiness*, p. 66.

16. Harry Emerson Fosdick, *The Meaning of Prayer*, p. 130.

17. Roger Hazelton, *The Root and Flower of Prayer*, p. 83.

18. George S. Stewart, *The Lower Levels of Prayer*, p. 92.

19. O. Hallesby, *Prayer*, p. 137.

20. Georgia Harkness, *Prayer and the Common Life*, p. 63.

21. Donald G. Bloesch, *The Struggle of Prayer*, p. 67. Copyright © 1980

by Donald G. Bloesch. Reprinted by permission of Harper & Row, Publishers, Inc.

22. Albert Wieand, *The Gospel of Prayer*, p. 193. Used by permission.

23. Norman Pittenger, *Praying Today*, pp. 44-45. Used by permission.

24. Ladislaus Boros, *Christian Prayer*, p. 26.

25. Jacob Agus, "The Meaning of Prayer," *Great Jewish Ideas*, ed. Abraham Millgram (Hudson, Mass.: Colonial Press, Inc., 1964), p. 223. Reprinted with permission from *Great Jewish Ideas* edited by Abraham E. Millgram, B'nai B'rith Great Book Series, Vol. 5, 1964, B'nai B'rith Commission on Adult Jewish Education.

26. Douglas Steere, *Dimensions of Prayer*, p. 50.

27. Harold Carter, *The Prayer Tradition of Black People*, pp. 65-66.

28. William Barclay, *Prayers for Young People*, p. 14. Copyright © 1963 by William Barclay. Reprinted by permission of Harper & Row, Publishers, Inc.

29. Leslie Weatherhead, *A Private House of Prayer* (Nashville: Abingdon Press, 1958), p. 24. Copyright © 1958 by Leslie D. Weatherhead. Used by permission of the publisher, Abingdon Press.

30. George A. Buttrick, *Prayer*, p. 83.

31. Hugh Warner, comp., *Daily Readings from William Temple*, p. 180.

Chapter 6 Intercession

1. Roger Hazelton, *The Root and Flower of Prayer*, p. 84.

2. John Casteel, *The Promise of Prayer*, pp. 76-77.

3. Mark Link, S.J., *Breakaway* (Allen, Tex.: Argus Communications, 1980), p. 77. Copyright © 1980 Argus Communications, Allen, Texas.

4. Roger Schutz, *The Rule of Taizé*, p. 18.

5. Thomas Kepler, comp., *The Evelyn Underhill Reader*, p. 165.

6. Olive Wyon, *Prayer*, p. 67.

7. Howard Thurman, *Disciplines of the Spirit*, p. 101.

8. Rufus M. Jones, *Rufus Jones Speaks to Our Time, An Anthology*, ed. Harry Emerson Fosdick (New York: Macmillan Inc., 1951), p. 156.

9. William Barclay, *A Spiritual Autobiography*, pp. 88-89. Used by permission.

10. Quoted in Harold Carter, *The Prayer Tradition of Black People*, p. 94.

11. Arthur Gossip, *In the Secret Place of the Most High*, p. 141.

12. Lance Webb, *The Art of Personal Prayer*, p. 92.

13. C. F. Andrews, *Christ and Prayer* (New York: Harper & Row, Publishers, Inc., 1937), p. 153.

14. Monica Furlong, *Contemplating Now* (Philadelphia: The Westminster Press, 1971), p. 69.

15. Charles Whiston, *Pray, A Study of Distinctively Christian Prayer*, p. 71. Used by permission.

16. Paul Tournier, *The Person Reborn*, trans. Edwin Hudson (New York: Harper & Row, Publishers, Inc., 1966) p. 228. Copyright © 1966 by Paul Tournier. Reprinted by permission of Harper & Row, Publishers, Inc.

17. C. S. Lewis, *Letters to Malcolm: Chiefly on Prayer*, p. 66.

18. E. Herman, *Creative Prayer*, p. 157. Reprinted by permission of Harper & Row, Publishers, Inc.

19. Frank Laubach, *Channels of Spiritual Power*, p. 51.

20. Flora Wuellner, *Prayer and the Living Christ*, pp. 110-111.

21. Harry Emerson Fosdick, *The Meaning of Prayer*, p. 192.

22. C. F. Andrews, *Christ and Prayer*, p. 136.

23. Georgia Harkness, *Prayer and the Common Life*, p. 80.

24. Albert Belden, *The Practice of Prayer* (New York: Harper & Row, Publishers, Inc., 1954), p. 43. Reprinted by permission of Harper & Row, Publishers, Inc.

25. Marjorie Holmes, *How Can I Find You, God?* (Garden City, N. Y.: Doubleday & Company, Inc., 1975), p. 122. Copyright © 1975 by Marjorie Holmes Mighell. Reprinted by permission of Doubleday & Company, Inc.

26. W. Graham Scroggie, *Method in Prayer*, p. 93.

27. Thomas Kepler, comp., *The Evelyn Underhill Reader*, p. 95.

28. H. Wayne Pipkin, *Christian Meditation, Its Art and Practice* (New York: Hawthorn Books, Inc., 1977), p. 107. Reprinted by permission of Hawthorn Properties, Elsevier-Dutton Publishing Co., Inc. Copyright © by H. Wayne Pipkin.

29. John Macquarrie, *The Humility of God*, p. 46.

30. Albert Schweitzer, *Memoirs of Childhood and Youth* (New York: Macmillan, Inc.), pp. 27-28.

Chapter 7 Silence

1. Dag Hammarskjöld, *Markings*, p. 156.

2. William Axling, *Kagawa*, p. 168. Copyright © 1932, 1946, by Harper & Row, Publishers, Inc. Reprinted by permission of Harper & Row, Publishers, Inc.

3. Thomas Troeger, *Rage! Reflect. Rejoice!*, p. 77.

4. Edgar N. Jackson, *Understanding Prayer* (Cleveland: The World Publishing Company, 1968), p. 128.

5. Anthony Bloom, *Beginning to Pray*, p. 58.

6. Carlo Carretto, *Letters from the Desert*, trans. Rose Mary Hancock (Marynoll, N. Y.: Orbis Books, 1972), p. 73.

7. Albert Belden, *The Practice of Prayer*, p. 85. Reprinted by permission of Harper & Row, Publishers, Inc.

8. Thomas R. Kelly, *A Testament of Devotion*, p. 75. Reprinted by permission of Harper & Row, Publishers, Inc.

9. Paul Tournier, *The Adventure of Living*, trans. Edwin Hudson (New York: Harper & Row, Publishers, Inc., 1965), p. 219. Copyright © 1965 by Edwin Hudson. Reprinted by permission of Harper & Row, Publishers, Inc.

10. Roger Schutz, *The Rule of Taizé*, p. 36.

11. Henri J. Nouwen, *Clowning in Rome*, p. 28. Copyright © 1979 by Henri J. M. Nouwen. Reprinted by permission of Doubleday & Company, Inc.

12. Wayne E. Oates, *Nurturing Silence in a Noisy Heart* (Garden City, N. Y.: Doubleday & Co., Inc., 1979), p. 33.

13. Oswald Chambers, *The Place of Help*, p. 111.

14. Ivan Illich, *Celebration of Awareness* (Garden City, N. Y.: Doubleday & Company, Inc., 1969), pp. 50-51. Copyright © 1970 by Ivan D. Illich. Reprinted by permission of Doubleday & Company, Inc.

15. Howard Thurman, *Disciplines of the Spirit*, p. 97.

16. E. Herman, *Creative Prayer*, p. 49. Reprinted by permission of Harper & Row, Publishers, Inc.

17. Thomas Merton, *The Climate of Monastic Prayer*, p. 122.

18. Donald G. Bloesch, *The Struggle of Prayer*, p. 54. Copyright © 1980 by Donald G. Bloesch. Reprinted by permission of Harper & Row, Publishers, Inc.

19. C. F. Andrews, *Christ and Prayer*, p. 97.

20. Wayne E. Oates, *Nurturing Silence in a Noisy Heart*, pp. 29-30.
21. Leslie Weatherhead, *A Private House of Prayer*, p. 69.
22. Quoted in Kermit Olsen, *First Steps in Prayer*, p. 101.
23. Dag Hammarskjöld, *Markings*, p. 83.
24. Howard Thurman, *The Centering Moment*, p. 85. Copyright © 1969 by Howard Thurman. Reprinted by permission of Harper & Row, Publishers, Inc.
25. Olive Wyon, *Prayer*, p. 55.
26. E. Stanley Jones, *Abundant Living* (Nashville: Abingdon Press, 1942), p. 253. Copyright renewal © 1970 by E. Stanley Jones. Used by permission of the publisher, Abingdon Press.
27. Albert Belden, *The Practice of Prayer*, p. 82. Reprinted by permission of Harper & Row, Publishers, Inc.
28. James E. Griffiss, *A Silent Path to God*, p. 22.
29. Thomas Troeger, *Rage! Reflect. Rejoice!*, pp. 58-59.
30. Dietrich Bonhoeffer, *Life Together*, p. 79.

Chapter 8 Persistence

1. John B. Magee, *Reality and Prayer*, p. 130.
2. Frederick Buechner, *Wishful Thinking, A Theological ABC*, p. 71. Copyright © 1973 by Frederick Buechner. Reprinted by permission of Harper & Row, Publishers, Inc.
3. Karl Rahner and Johann Baptist Metz, *The Courage To Pray*, p. 12.
4. P. T. Forsyth, *The Soul of Prayer*, p. 12.
5. Harry Emerson Fosdick, *The Meaning of Prayer*, p. 128.
6. William Toohey, *Life After Birth*, pp. 61-62.
7. Donald G. Bloesch, *The Struggle of Prayer*, p. 81. Copyright © 1980 by Donald G. Bloesch. Reprinted by permission of Harper & Row, Publishers, Inc.
8. Alexander Whyte, *Lord, Teach Us to Pray* (New York: George H. Doran Company, n.d.), p. 216.
9. Jacques Ellul, *Prayer and Modern Man*, p. 162.
10. Leslie Weatherhead, *A Private House of Prayer*, p. 28.
11. Douglas Steere, *Dimensions of Prayer*, p. 111.
12. Karl Rahner and Johann Baptist Metz, *The Courage to Pray*, p. 13.
13. Harold Carter, *The Prayer Tradition of Black People*, p. 98.
14. O. Hallesby, *Prayer*, p. 110.
15. Thomas Troeger, *Rage! Reflect. Rejoice!*, p. 54.
16. Donald G. Bloesch, *The Struggle of Prayer*, p. 76. Copyright © 1980 by Donald G. Bloesch. Reprinted by permission of Harper & Row, Publishers, Inc.
17. Alexander Whyte, *Lord, Teach Us to Pray*, p. 204.
18. Hugh Warner, comp., *Daily Readings from William Temple*, p. 117.
19. P. T. Forsyth, *The Soul of Prayer*, p. 91.
20. Samuel Zwemer, *Taking Hold of God* (Grand Rapids, Mich.: The Zondervan Corp., 1936), pp. 32-33.
21. Frank Laubach, *Prayer Diary* (Old Tappan, N.J.: Fleming H. Revell Company, 1964), p. 38.
22. C. F. Andrews, *Christ and Prayer*, p. 89.
23. Thomas Kepler, comp., *The Evelyn Underhill Reader*, p. 166.
24. E. Stanley Jones, *Abundant Living*, p. 231.
25. Alexis Carrel, *Prayer*, pp. 25-26.
26. Oswald Chambers, *The Place of Help*, pp. 110-111.

27. William Toohey, *Life After Birth*, p. 62.
28. Karl Rahner and Johann Baptist Metz, *The Courage to Pray*, p. 27.
29. Leslie Weatherhead, *A Private House of Prayer*, p. 28.
30. Martin Luther King, Jr., *Strength to Love*, p. 50.
31. William Hull, "Prayer: Human and Divine," *The Twentieth Century Pulpit*, Vol. II., ed. James Cox (Nashville: Abingdon Press, 1981), p. 103.

Chapter 9 Communion

1. Harry Emerson Fosdick, *The Meaning of Prayer*, p. 32.
2. Harry Emerson Fosdick, ed., *Rufus Jones Speaks to Our Time, An Anthology*, p. 151.
3. Kosuke Koyama, *50 Meditations* (Maryknoll, N. Y.: Orbis Books, 1979), pp. 9-10.
4. *The Wisdom of Heschel*, selected by Ruth Marcus Goodhill, p. 210. Reprinted by permission of Farrar, Straus and Giroux, Inc. Copyright © 1970, 1972, 1975 by Sylvia Heschel, Executrix of the Estate of Abraham Joshua Heschel.
5. Karl Barth, *Prayer According to the Catechisms of the Reformation*, p. 23.
6. L. Robert Keck, *The Spirit of Synergy: God's Power and You* (Nashville: Abingdon Press, 1978), p. 106. Copyright © 1978 by L. Robert Keck. Used by permission of the publisher, Abingdon Press.
7. Lance Webb, *The Art of Personal Prayer*, p. 155.
8. P. T. Forsyth, *The Soul of Prayer*, p. 16.
9. Howard Thurman, *Disciplines of the Spirit*, p. 95.
10. Thomas Kepler, comp., *The Evelyn Underhill Reader*, p. 165.
11. Harold Carter, *The Prayer Tradition of Black People*, p. 53.
12. Robert Speer, *A Christian's Habits*, p. 16.
13. Alexis Carrel, *Prayer*, p. 26.
14. Albert Belden, *The Practice of Prayer*, p. 26. Reprinted by permission of Harper & Row, Publishers, Inc.
15. Oswald Chambers, *The Place of Help*, p. 113.
16. E. Herman, *Creative Prayer*, p. 161. Reprinted by permission of Harper & Row, Publishers, Inc.
17. Henri J. Nouwen, *Clowning in Rome*, p. 70. Copyright © 1979 by Henri J. M. Nouwen. Reprinted by permission of Doubleday & Company, Inc.
18. P. T. Forsyth, *The Soul of Prayer*, p. 26.
19. Thomas Kepler, comp., *The Evelyn Underhill Reader*, p. 172.
20. Martin Luther King, Jr., *Stride Toward Freedom* (New York: Harper & Row, Publishers, Inc., 1958), pp. 134-135. Copyright © 1958 by Martin Luther King, Jr. Reprinted by permission of Harper & Row, Publishers, Inc.
21. Thomas Troeger, *Rage! Reflect. Rejoice!*, p. 76.
22. John Wishart, *The Fact of Prayer* (Old Tappan, N. J.: Fleming H. Revell Co., 1927), p. 60.
23. Alexis Carrel, *Prayer*, p. 18.
24. Howard Thurman, *The Centering Moment*, p. 27. Copyright © 1969 by Howard Thurman. Reprinted by permission of Harper & Row, Publishers, Inc.
25. L. Robert Keck, *The Spirit of Synergy*, p. 127.
26. Donald G. Bloesch, *The Struggle of Prayer*, p. 163. Copyright © 1980 by Donald G. Bloesch. Reprinted by permission of Harper & Row, Publishers, Inc.

27. Henri J. Nouwen, *Clowning in Rome*, p. 82. Copyright © 1979 by Henri J. M. Nouwen. Reprinted by permission of Doubleday & Company, Inc.
28. Albert Belden, *The Practice of Prayer*, p. 25. Reprinted by permission of Harper & Row, Publishers, Inc.
29. Pierre Teilhard de Chardin, *Writings in Times of War*, trans. René Hague (New York: Harper & Row, Publishers, Inc., 1965), p. 147.
30. Edward J. Farrell, *Prayer Is a Hunger*, p. 18.

Chapter 10 Surrender

1. George A. Buttrick, *Prayer*, p. 225.
2. William Toohey, *Life After Birth*, pp. 63-64.
3. E. Herman, *Creative Prayer*, p. 119. Reprinted by permission of Harper & Row, Publishers, Inc.
4. Mother Teresa, *A Gift for God*, p. 39. Copyright © 1975 by Mother Teresa, Missionaries of Charity. Reprinted by permission of Harper & Row, Publishers, Inc.
5. Clarence Jordan, *Sermon on the Mount*, p. 89.
6. *The Wisdom of Heschel*, selected by Ruth Marcus Goodhill, p. 211. Reprinted by permission of Farrar, Straus and Giroux, Inc. Copyright © 1970, 1972, 1975 by Sylvia Heschel, Executrix of the Estate of Abraham Joshua Heschel.
7. Olive Wyon, *Prayer*, p. 26.
8. E. Stanley Jones, *Abundant Living*, p. 225.
9. Dag Hammarskjöld, *Markings*, p. 69.
10. John B. Magee, *Reality and Prayer*, p. 140.
11. Thomas R. Kelly, *A Testament of Devotion*, p. 61. Reprinted by permission of Harper & Row, Publishers, Inc.
12. Martin Buber, *The Way of Response*: edited by Nahum N. Glatzer (New York: Schocken Books, Inc., 1966), p. 67. Reprinted by permission of Schocken Books, Inc.
13. P. T. Forsyth, *The Soul of Prayer*, p. 85.
14. Karl Rahner, *On Prayer* (New York: Paulist Press, 1968), p. 82.
15. Lance Webb, *The Art of Personal Prayer*, p. 114.
16. C. S. Lewis, *Letters to Malcolm: Chiefly on Prayer*, p. 116.
17. Thomas Merton, *The Climate of Monastic Prayer*, p. 102.
18. Flora Wuellner, *Prayer and the Living Christ*, p. 78.
19. John B. Magee, *Reality and Prayer*, pp. 174-175.
20. Thomas Troeger, *Rage! Reflect. Rejoice!*, p. 78.
21. Georgia Harkness, *Prayer and the Common Life*, p. 84.
22. *The Wisdom of Heschel*, selected by Ruth Marcus Goodhill, p. 207. Reprinted by permission of Farrar, Straus and Giroux, Inc. Copyright © 1970, 1972, 1975 by Sylvia Heschel, Executrix of the Estate of Abraham Joshua Heschel.
23. Thomas Kepler, comp., *The Evelyn Underhill Reader*, p. 97.
24. Oswald Chambers, *The Place of Help*, p. 20.
25. Frank Laubach, *Prayer Diary*, p. 7.
26. Mother Teresa, *A Gift for God*, p. 78. Copyright © 1975 by Mother Teresa, Missionaries of Charity. Reprinted by permission of Harper & Row, Publishers, Inc.
27. Kermit Olsen, *First Steps in Prayer*, p. 99.
28. Alexis Carrel, *Prayer*, p. 23.
29. Albert Belden, *The Practice of Prayer*, p. 35. Reprinted by permission of Harper & Row, Publishers, Inc.

30. Howard Thurman, *The Centering Moment*, p. 125. Copyright © 1969 by Howard Thurman. Reprinted by permission of Harper & Row, Publishers, Inc.

31. "Letter to a friend, 1934," quoted in *Wit and Wisdom of Good Pope John*, collected by Henri Fesquet (New York: P. J. Kenedy & Sons, 1964), p. 179.

Chapter 11 Recollection

1. Alexander Whyte, *Lord, Teach Us to Pray*, p. 238.
2. Morton T. Kelsey, *The Other Side of Silence*, p. 197.
3. Mark Link, *Breakaway*, pp. 38-39.
4. E. Stanley Jones, *Abundant Living*, p. 229.
5. Edward J. Farrell, *Prayer Is a Hunger*, p. 23.
6. Paul Tournier, *The Adventure of Living*, pp. 212-214.
7. Frank Laubach, *Channels of Spiritual Power*, p. 145.
8. Mark Link, *Breakaway*, p. 35.
9. John B. Magee, *Reality and Prayer*, p. 78.
10. Pope John XXIII, *Journal of a Soul*, p. 61.
11. Morton T. Kelsey, *The Other Side of Silence*, p. 200.
12. Edgar N. Jackson, *Understanding Prayer*, p. 165.
13. Thomas Merton, *The Climate of Monastic Prayer*, p. 30-32.
14. J. Neville Ward, *The Use of Praying*, p. 114.
15. Harold Carter, *The Prayer Tradition of Black People*, p. 120.
16. Charles Whiston, *Pray, A Study of Distinctively Christian Praying*, p. 110. Used by permission.
17. John S. Bonnell, *Psychology for Pastor and People*, pp. 107-108. Reprinted by permission of Harper & Row, Publishers, Inc.
18. John B. Coburn, *Prayer and Personal Religion*, p. 70.
19. Donald G. Bloesch, *The Struggle of Prayer*, pp. 20-21. Copyright © 1980 by Donald G. Bloesch. Reprinted by permission of Harper & Row, Publishers, Inc.
20. Frank Laubach, *Prayer Diary*, p. 9.
21. John Yungblut, *Rediscovering Prayer*, p. 68.
22. Charles Whiston, *Pray, A Study of Distinctively Christian Praying*, pp. 107-109. Used by permission.
23. Alexander Whyte, *Lord, Teach Us to Pray*, p. 251.
24. Norman Pittenger, *Praying Today*, p. 61. Used by permission.
25. Jacob Agus, "The Meaning of Prayer," *Great Jewish Ideas*, p. 229.
26. Andrew M. Greeley, *Letters to Nancy* (New York: Sheed and Ward, imprint of Andrews & McMeel, Inc., Fairway, Kans., 1964), p. 153.
27. Howard Thurman, *The Centering Moment*, p. 32. Copyright © 1969 by Howard Thurman. Reprinted by permission of Harper & Row, Publishers, Inc.
28. Patrick Jacquemont, "Is Action Prayer?," *The Prayer Life*, ed. Christian Duquoc and Claude Geffré (New York: Herder and Herder, 1972), p. 49.
29. Edward J. Farrell, *Prayer Is a Hunger*, p. 30.

Chapter 12 Action

1. Norman Pittenger, *Praying Today*, pp. 106-107. Used by permission.
2. Olive Wyon, *Prayer*, p. 59.
3. Dag Hammarskjöld, *Markings*, p. 122.
4. Thomas Merton, *The Climate of Monastic Prayer*, p. 149.
5. Hugh Warner, comp., *Daily Readings from William Temple*, pp. 34-35.

6. Nikos Kazantzakis, *Report to Greco*, p. 306.
7. Walter Rauschenbusch, *Prayers of the Social Awakening*, p. 12.
8. Frank Laubach, *Channels of Spiritual Power*, p. 174.
9. Jacques Ellul, *Prayer and Modern Man*, p. 173.
10. Harry Emerson Fosdick, *The Meaning of Prayer*, pp. 147-148.
11. Donald G. Bloesch, *The Struggle of Prayer*, p. 136. Copyright © 1980 by Donald G. Bloesch. Reprinted by permission of Harper & Row, Publishers, Inc.
12. E. Stanley Jones, *Abundant Living*, p. 231.
13. Mother Teresa, *A Gift for God*, p. 82-83. Copyright © 1975 by Mother Teresa, Missionaries of Charity. Reprinted by permission of Harper & Row, Publishers, Inc.
14. Michael H. Crosby, *Thy Will Be Done, Praying the Our Father as Subversive Activity*, p. 55.
15. William Toohey, *Life After Birth*, p. 65.
16. Louis Evely, *Our Prayer* (New York: Herder and Herder, 1970) p. 106.
17. Dietrich Bonhoeffer, *Life Together*, p. 88.
18. Carlo Carretto, *Letters from the Desert*, pp. 24-25.
19. Thomas R. Kelly, *A Testament of Devotion*, p. 123. Reprinted by permission of Harper & Row, Publishers, Inc.
20. Thomas Merton, *The Climate of Monastic Prayer*, p. 55.
21. Donald G. Bloesch, *The Struggle of Prayer*, p. 143. Copyright © 1980 by Donald G. Bloesch. Reprinted by permission of Harper & Row, Publishers, Inc.
22. Paul Tournier, *The Person Reborn*, trans. Edwin Herdson, p. 141. Copyright © 1966 by Paul Tournier. Reprinted by permission of Harper & Row, Publishers, Inc.
23. Louis Evely, Our *Prayer*, p. 109.
24. Martin Luther King, Jr., *The Trumphet of Conscience* (New York: Harper & Row, Publishers, Inc., 1967), p. 59. Copyright © 1967 by Martin Luther King, Jr. Reprinted by permission of Harper & Row, Publishers, Inc.
25. Helmut Thielicke, *Being a Christian When the Chips Are Down*, trans. H. George Anderson (Philadelphia: Fortress Press, 1979), p. 101.
26. William Barclay, *Prayers for Young People*, p. 17. Copyright © 1963 by William Barclay. Reprinted by permission of Harper & Row, Publishers, Inc.
27. John Macquarrie, *The Humility of God*, p. 44.
28. P.T. Forsyth, *The Soul of Prayer*, p. 27.
29. L. Robert Keck, *The Spirit of Synergy*, p. 106.
30. Henri J. M. Nouwen, *With Open Hands* (Notre Dame, Ind.: Ave Maria Press, 1972), p. 157. Used by permission of the publisher.
31. P. T. Forsyth, *The Soul of Prayer*, p. 64.

Index by Authors

the Journey. Waco, Tex.: Word, Inc., 1976.
King, Martin Luther, Jr.   21, 85, 92, 121
Strength to Love. New York: Harper & Row, Publishers, Inc., 1963.
Stride Toward Freedom. New York: Harper & Row, Publishers, Inc., 1958.
The Trumpet of Conscience. New York: Harper & Row, Publishers, Inc., 1967.
Koyma, Kosuke   88
50 Meditations. Maryknoll, N.Y.: Orbis Books, 1979.

Laubach, Frank   11, 49, 62, 82-83, 101, 107, 111, 117
Channels of Spiritual Power. Old Tappan, N.J.: Fleming H. Revell Co., 1954.
Prayer Diary. Old Tappan, N.J.: Fleming H. Revell Co., 1964.
L'Engle, Madeleine   7
"The Gift of Prayer," *A. D.* April, 1980.
Lewis, C. S.   23, 30, 50, 62, 99
Letters to Malcolm: Chiefly on Prayer. New York: Harcourt Brace Jovanovich, Inc., 1964.
Link, Mark   58, 106, 107
Breakaway. Allen, Tex.: Argus Communications, 1980.

Macquarrie, John   48, 65, 122
The Humility of God. Neperville, Ill.: SCM Book Club, 1978.
Magee, John B.   31, 35, 50, 77, 97, 99-100, 107
Reality and Prayer. Nashville: Abingdon Press, 1957.
Merton, Thomas   30, 71, 99, 109, 116, 120
The Climate of Monastic Prayer. Kalamazoo, Mich.: Cistercian Publications, 1969.

Nouwen, Henri J. M.   22, 70, 91, 93-94, 122
Clowning in Rome. Garden City, N.Y.: Doubleday & Co., Inc., Image Books, 1979.

With Open Hands. Notre Dame, Ind.: Ave Maria Press, 1972.

Oates, Wayne E.   70, 72
Nurturing Silence in a Noisy Heart. Garden City, N.Y.: Doubleday & Co., Inc., 1979.
O'Connor, Elizabeth   11
Journey Inward, Journey Outward. New York: Harper & Row, Publishers, Inc., 1968.
Olsen, Kermit   37-38, 73, 102
First Steps in Prayer. Old Tappan, N.J.: Fleming H. Revell Co., 1942.

Pipkin, H. Wayne   65
Christian Meditation, Its Art and Practice. New York: Hawthorn Books, Inc., 1977.
Pittenger, W. Norman   21, 42, 52-53, 112, 115
Praying Today. Grand Rapids, Mich.: Wm. B. Eerdmans Publishing Co., 1974.

Quoist, Michel   39
Prayers. Trans. Agnes M. Forsyth and Anne Marie de Commaille. New York: Sheed and Ward, 1963. (Imprint of Andrews & McMeel, Inc., Fairway, Kans.).

Rahner, Karl   78, 98
On Prayer. New York: Paulist Press, 1968.
Rahner, Karl; and Metz, Johann B.   47, 78, 80, 84
The Courage to Pray. New York: The Crossroad Publishing Co., 1981.
Rauschenbusch, Walter   21, 116
Prayers of the Social Awakening. New York: The Pilgrim Press, 1910.
Read, David   19
Holy Common Sense. Nashville: Abingdon Press, 1966.

Schutz, Roger   12, 58, 69
The Rule of Taizé. France: The Communaute de Taizé, 1961.
Schweitzer, Albert   65-66
Memoirs of Childhood and Youth. New York: Macmillan, Inc., 1949.

Lord, Teach Us to Pray. New York: George H. Doran Co., n.d.

Wieand, Albert   42, 52
The Gospel of Prayer. Grand Rapids, Mich.: Wm. B. Eerdmans Publishing Co., 1953.

Williams, H. A.   10
The Simplicity of Prayer. Philadelphia: Fortress Press, 1977.

Wishart, John   92
The Fact of Prayer. Old Tappan, N.J.: Fleming H. Revell Co., 1927.

Wojtyla, Karol (Pope John Paul II)   14-15
Sign of Contradiction. New York: The Crossroad Publishing Co., 1979.

Wuellner, Flora   31, 48, 62-63, 99
Prayer and the Living Christ. Nashville: Abingdon Press, 1969.

Wyon, Olive   17, 58, 74, 96-97, 115
Prayer. Philadelphia: Fortress Press, 1960.

Yungblut, John   17, 111
Rediscovering Prayer. New York: The Seabury Press, Inc., 1972.

Zwemer, Samuel   82
Taking Hold of God. Grand Rapids, Mich.: The Zondervan Corp., 1936.

FastCat 200-579   3/93

DATE DUE

MAY 9 '83			
JUN 30 '83			
OCT 18 '83			
DEC 21 '84			
DEC 19			
JUL 24 '87			
SEP. 24 1998			